General Edi~~~~~~~~~~~~~~~~~~~~~~~~~~~~~~
of Stirling) & Professor Suheil Bushrui (*American*
University of Beirut)

William Congreve

THE WAY OF
THE WORLD

Notes by Bo Jeffares

BA (READING) MA (COURTAULD INSTITUTE,
UNIVERSITY OF LONDON) PH D (DUBLIN)

LONGMAN
YORK PRESS

YORK PRESS
Immeuble Esseily, Place Riad Solh, Beirut.

LONGMAN GROUP UK LIMITED
Longman House,
Burnt Mill,
Harlow,
Essex

First published 1983
Reprinted 1988

ISBN 0-582-02320-3

Produced by Longman Group (FE) Ltd
Printed in Hong Kong

Contents

Contents

Part 1

Introduction

The life of William Congreve

William Congreve was born in Bardsey, a Yorkshire village north of Leeds, in 1670, but he grew up in Ireland where his father served first as commander of the garrison at Youghal, County Cork, moving from there to Carrickfergus and then to Kilkenny in County Kildare. William was sent to Kilkenny College, an excellent school supported by the distinguished Ormonde family. He then went to Trinity College Dublin, the University founded by Queen Elizabeth in 1591. In 1688 most of the staff and students went to England because of the dangerous political situation in Ireland. At first Congreve stayed at the family seat in Staffordshire, then went to London to become a student of law at the Middle Temple in 1691. In that year, after William's victories over James II in Ireland had stabilised conditions and established the political power of Protestantism there, Congreve's father returned to Ireland, to become agent for the Earl of Cork.

In London Congreve preferred drama to law. He was a good classical scholar and interested in translation; his poems and translations impressed the dramatist, poet and critic John Dryden (1631–1700) who included some of them in a collection of miscellaneous poems called *Examen Poeticum* (1693). In 1692 Congreve's novel *Incognita* was published: its plot was worked out on the lines of dramatic models, and the following year he finished his first play, *The Old Batchelor*. Dryden, who was most influential, thought well of it and helped Congreve to polish it; it was performed in 1693 and was extremely successful.

The actress Anne Bracegirdle established her fame by playing the role of Araminta in this play; she became 'the darling of the theatre'. Congreve, who was obviously greatly in love with her, created his subsequent heroines with 'our friend Venus'—a part she played in his masque *The Judgement of Paris*—in mind. She was accompanied by a good cast in *The Old Batchelor*, notably the actors Thomas Betterton and Thomas Dogget.

There followed *The Double-Dealer*, a sombre play which was not so successful—much to the annoyance of Congreve and Dryden who had expected a better reception for what remains a powerful piece of drama. Congreve's next play, *Love for Love*, however, was much more successful when it was staged in 1695. It was performed by a company managed by Congreve and his fellow dramatist Sir John Vanbrugh (1664–1726), who was also a celebrated architect, the designer of Blenheim Palace and Castle Howard. It was intended that Congreve should write a play a year for the new dramatic company, but he did not manage to fulfil this expectation. His next play *The Mourning Bride* was a tragedy which proved popular when it was staged in 1697.

The next year, 1698, saw the publication of the Rev. Jeremy Collier's pamphlet *A Short View of the Immorality and Profaneness of the English Stage together with the Sense of Ambiguity upon this argument*. This attack on the morality of the contemporary theatre reflected a change in the attitude of the audience. Although Congreve replied to it his reply was not very effective. He himself realised this, and indeed mentioned the matter in the Dedication to his next play, *The Way of the World* (1700), saying that the fact that his comedy succeeded on the stage was almost beyond his expectations because little of it was prepared for 'that general taste' which had become predominant in the audience.

The following year he completed his masque, *The Judgement of Paris*, and then, after collaborating with Vanbrugh and another writer, Walsh, in a farce called *Monsieur de Pourceaugnac, or, Squire Trelooby*, he wrote no more for the theatre. At the age of thirty, then, he ceased to be a dramatist, and at thirty-five he gave up his managership in the company which he and Vanbrugh had first established in 1704.

Instead of writing he had become a public servant: this career began in 1695 when he was commissioner for licensing lackey coaches; next he was collector of customs at Poole, in 1700–2, and then commissioner for wine licences in 1705. When the Whigs lost power to the Tories he was afraid he would be deprived of these official posts, but his friend Jonathan Swift (1667–1745), who had been at Kilkenny College and Trinity College Dublin with him, interceded on his behalf with the Tories and helped to have him confirmed in his posts. When the Whigs returned to power in 1714, Congreve gave up his commissionership for wine licences, and was appointed instead to a post in the customs in London. He also became Secretary for Jamaica. These posts, which he held till his death, made him a wealthy man.

By 1710 Congreve's health had deteriorated; he was almost blind with cataracts and 'never rid of the gout'; his friendship with Mrs Bracegirdle seems to have come to an end, and he withdrew from a large part of his social life—his friends included, besides Swift, John Gay (1685–1732), Alexander Pope (1688–1744), Sir Richard Steele (1672–1729) and Lady Mary Wortley Montagu (1698–1762). Despite his bad health he remained a cheerful man; he was deeply fond of his friends who returned his affection. After 1705 he became a close friend of Henrietta, the second Duchess of Marlborough, and was probably the father of her youngest daughter Mary, Duchess of Leeds (to whom his estate, left to the Duchess, came intact after the latter's death). He and the Duchess went to Bath in 1728, hoping that his health would benefit, but he grew weaker and died in January 1729. He was buried in Westminster Abbey.

The comedy of manners

The Puritans closed the theatres in England in 1642. When Charles II was restored to the throne in 1660 he encouraged the revival of drama. Two companies were given patents and under the direction of Sir William Davenant (1606–68) and Thomas Killigrew (1612–83) were soon in action. The plays performed reflected the taste of an aristocratic audience: there were high-flown 'heroic' plays and tearful tragedies, and there were also the comedies: dashing, witty, coarse, cynical, satiric, sardonic. The comedies voiced a reaction against puritanism and the sexual repression it had attempted to enforce. Fashionable intrigue, sex, marriage and adultery were treated with cynicism, with worldly wit and a sense of the comedy of life. The characters in the plays no doubt owed much to the courtiers, the wits, the men-about-town as well as to ladies of fashion, citizens' wives and country girls. But there were other sources for the playwright to draw upon than goings-on at the court. Many authors plundered earlier work, some going as far back as classical writings such as the plays of Plautus (c. 254–184BC) and Terence (c. 190–159BC), who had themselves been influenced by earlier Greek comedies such as those of Menander (c. 342–292BC). The plays of Ben Jonson (1572–1637) and those of Beaumont (1584–1616) and Fletcher (1579–1625) were used, as well as Spanish and French comedies. Molière (1622–73), in particular, had a strong influence upon the English comic writers, who often blended material from different plays with their own. However, life in London, at the court especially, was probably the main source for the material of this flourishing period of comedy. Fashionable life, with its sophisticated pursuit of sensuous pleasure, provided material in plenty for the authors, who came from a variety of backgrounds: some of them were men-about-town who wrote with an elegant, insouciant ease, others were professional authors such as John Dryden, others again theatre managers or actors.

After the Restoration the actors had been joined by actresses (women's parts had earlier been played by boys), whose private lives created plenty of interest for the audience—the King's relationships, for instance, with the actresses Nell Gwynn and Moll Davis were notorious. Another development was the use of movable scenery; and this combined with a larger forestage to add visual interest as well as allowing more flexible action. Besides admiring the attractions of the actresses the audience often created its own amusements—witty comments were frequently hurled at the plays, and oranges at the players, if the play did not please. Indeed the audience was mobile: its members often moved from one playhouse to the other if they were not sufficiently interested by the play or the women in the theatre.

There were predictable ingredients in the comedies: conflicts between youth and age, between parents and children. Inheritance and debts caused some of the problems to be solved—and the financial affairs of the characters were usually neatly arranged by the end of a play. There were flippant remarks about marriage, intrigues informed by intelligence, and witty gallantry and badinage. There was a good deal of deceit, and contrasts between sophisticated and naive characters from city and country respectively. Usually lovers' problems added to the complexity of the plot, which also gave scope to clever, impertinent servants; and there was often an amusing element of farce included. The exposure of pretence, the abandonment of false identities, often led to satisfactory solutions. What is remarkable is that so much good drama could be created in these conditions: wit and wisdom—admittedly often very worldly wisdom—were to be found in the satire of the comic writers. There was an underlying seriousness in some of these authors who were obviously disturbed by the current immorality and cheap cynicism.

The nature of Restoration comedy changed, as was to be expected. It reached its supreme achievement of wit and elegance in *The Way of the World*. The play was first staged forty years after the Restoration; but by that time the audience had moved from aristocratic attitudes to those of the middle class. Jeremy Collier's attack on the immorality of the drama had expressed a reaction to the libertinism and vice which had been ingredients of the first Restoration plays and had remained a strong element in their successors. The change in the nature of comedy can be traced in the plays of George Farquhar (1678–1707). His two best-known plays which are deservedly popular, *The Recruiting Officer* (1706) and *The Beaux' Stratagem* (1707), moved their action from the capital, London, to the provinces and in doing so portrayed a simpler but kinder society. True, the plots revolve around the unsatisfactory nature of marriage, just as William Wycherley's (1640–1716) coarser plays had done earlier, dealing with this institution when based not upon love but upon alliances satisfactory from the point of view of money, land and family. It was the parents who decided what was satisfactory, but the results were often not happy for the husband or wife, as *The Beaux' Stratagem* makes clear. *The Recruiting Officer* also deals with marriage, but from a different point of view. The heroine Sylvia plays a 'breeches' part, disguising herself as an army officer as part of her campaign to marry the man she loves (a thing which appeared impossible to her father after his son died and Sylvia had become his heiress).

Farquhar's comedy was gentler than earlier plays; it was a step on the way to sentimental comedy, which offered more optimistic answers to the problems of threatened marriages. Colley Cibber's (1671–1757) play *The Careless Husband* (1705) illustrated how far the taste of the audience had changed when one of the characters remarked that 'the stage hardly dare show a vicious person for fear of being called profane for exposing him'. The change in taste was complete by the time of Sir Richard Steele (1672–1729) who disapproved of the earlier comedies of manners. He thought, for instance, that George Etherege's (?1634–?91) *The Man of Mode* (1676) was 'a perfect contradiction of good manners', and that Edward Ravenscroft's (1644–1704) *The London Cuckolds* (1682) was the 'most rank play' that ever succeeded. Steele's own plays were full of the domestic virtues, with cosy happy endings which pleased the new audience. In *The Conscious Lovers* (1722) he had one of his characters, Mr Sealand, a merchant, assert the achievements and the importance of the merchant class. Comedy had moved a long way from the early Restoration plays where the citizens, the often puritanical 'cits', were presented as an object of mirth to an aristocratic audience.

A note on the text

The Way of the World was first published by Jacob Tonson, London, in 1700; a second edition followed in 1706. The text was also included in *The Works*, 3 vols, 1710; this was reprinted as the second edition, 1717. The third edition, 2 vols, 1719–20, was 'revis'd by the author'. In *The Works* the text of the play is divided into a very large number of scenes beginning and ending with the entrances and exits of characters. The text used in the preparation of these Notes is that given in William Congreve, *Incognita and The Way of the World*, Edward Arnold, London, 1966.

Part 2

Summaries

of THE WAY OF THE WORLD

A general summary

The plot of *The Way of the World* may seem complicated at a first reading. A family tree will help you to identify the different characters:

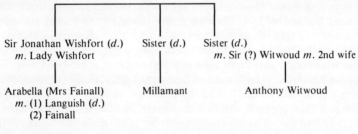

Sir Jonathan Wishfort (*d*.)   Sister (*d*.)   Sister (*d*.)
  m. Lady Wishfort   *m*. Sir (?) Witwoud *m*. 2nd wife

Arabella (Mrs Fainall)   Millamant   Anthony Witwoud
  m. (1) Languish (*d*.)
     (2) Fainall

d. = deceased
m. = married

In addition to the ageing coquette Lady Wishfort, her daughter Arabella (Mrs Fainall), and her niece Millamant, the other characters include Mirabell, who wishes to marry Millamant; Mrs Marwood, with whom Arabella's husband Fainall has an adulterous relationship; Petulant, who, like Anthony Witwoud, is a follower of Millamant. There are also Waitwell, Mirabell's servant, who is married to Foible, Lady Wishfort's maid, and Mincing, Mrs Millamant's maid.

The Way of the World begins with Fainall and Mirabell in a conversation which tells us something of the past relationships between the characters in the play. These two are fashionable men-about-town, involved with the Wishfort family, Fainall being married to Arabella, Lady Wishfort's daughter, and Mirabell wanting to marry Millamant. Mirabell has, however, paid attentions to Millamant's aunt Lady Wishfort, but the false nature of these advances has been exposed by Mrs Marwood, and this has, not unnaturally, enraged Lady Wishfort, who—at fifty-five—had been flattered by the attentions of a young man like Mirabell. Mirabell had acted thus to conceal his love for Millamant. Half of Millamant's fortune depends upon Lady Wishfort's approving her marriage. The play is partly about the current situation where the financial security of the young depended upon the whims of the older generation: it also deals with the fact that a wife's property was at her husband's disposal, and ultimately it considers how a marriage can work well as well as badly. There is another complication in that Mirabell compromised Mrs Fainall when she was a widow, and arranged her second marriage to Fainall, who married her for her money.

The information supplied in the opening conversation is vital to the subsequent working of the plot, though its purpose is not immediately clear. For instance, Mirabell asks if his servant Waitwell has married Lady Wishfort's servant Foible. He has let it be known, through the gossips, that he has an uncle who comes between him and his estate; if the uncle should marry and have a child Mirabell may be disinherited— the story is known to Petulant, and to Witwoud, the would-be wits (who are balanced against the genuine wits, Mirabell and Fainall). These are two strands in Mirabell's plot: against it will be set the plot concocted by Fainall and Mrs Marwood, also to gain control over Lady Wishfort, who can herself—through the provisions of a will— control Millamant's marriage and fortune and can also affect her own daughter's fortune, and thus the state of her marriage.

The second act opens with a conversation between Mrs Fainall and Mrs Marwood, who reveals her hatred of Mirabell. The conversation which follows, between Mrs Marwood and Fainall, shows us how he resents his mistress having told Lady Wishfort about Mirabell's deception, for, he says, had Mirabell married Millamant without Lady Wishfort's consent half Millamant's money would have come to Lady Wishfort, and, when she died, to her daughter, Mrs Fainall, his wife. The next conversation between Mirabell and Mrs Fainall shows that Mirabell had been Mrs Fainall's lover in the past, and then lets us know of his plot to get Lady Wishfort to marry his uncle. This role is to be played by Mirabell's servant Waitwell who will pretend to be Sir Rowland: since Mirabell does not trust him, Waitwell's marriage to Foible will allow Mirabell (if Lady Wishfort marries the supposed uncle) later to release Lady Wishfort from this marriage (by producing a certificate of Waitwell's previous marriage), on condition she agrees to Mirabell's marrying Millamant and gives up her claim to half of Millamant's fortune.

Millamant enters with Witwoud and her servant Mincing. After some general repartee Millamant and Mirabell are left alone, and she makes it clear that she knows of his device to gain Lady Wishfort's consent to their marriage. After she leaves, the act ends with Waitwell and Foible talking to Mirabell, whose scheme seems well under way.

The third act opens with Lady Wishfort at her toilette. She is visited by Mrs Marwood and then Foible arrives to further Mirabell's plans. Lady Wishfort is obviously taken with the idea of the supposed Sir Rowland. After she leaves Foible tells Mrs Fainall, who has come in, that all is going well, but she is overheard by Mrs Marwood who later suggests to Lady Wishfort that Millamant should marry Sir Willful Witwoud. Later Millamant and Mrs Marwood indulge in raillery, carried on with Witwoud and Petulant, and then with Sir Willful Witwoud. The plot is advanced in a dialogue between Fainall and Mrs Marwood, who suggests that he should denounce his wife's conduct to her mother, Lady Wishfort, and that Lady Wishfort will then agree to anything he demands. Fainall says that should his relationship with Mrs Marwood be discovered he already has a deed of settlement of the best part of his wife's estate which he will share with Mrs Marwood.

The fourth act opens with Lady Wishfort's preparations for a visit from the supposed Sir Rowland. After a brief scene between Millamant and her cousin, Mrs Fainall, Sir Willful Witwoud enters to pay court to Millamant, but proves too tongue-tied to advance his cause. A magnificent dialogue between Millamant and Mirabell follows, in which they agree how they will conduct themselves in marriage. Witwoud comes in from dining and is followed by a very drunk Petulant, and then by Lady Wishfort and Sir Willful (who is also very drunk). After the drunks leave, singing, the supposed Sir Rowland pays court to or rather is courted by Lady Wishfort. Prompted by Foible he manages to persuade her that a letter from Mrs Marwood, telling Lady Wishfort that 'Sir Rowland' is an impostor, has been written by Mirabell. He also persuades her to agree to marry him.

In the opening of the fifth act Lady Wishfort accuses Foible of her part in the plot, and is all the more enraged to hear that Waitwell was already married to Foible; she tells Foible that Waitwell is in gaol and that she will put Foible there presently. Mrs Marwood and Fainall have told her of Mirabell's plot. Then we hear that Fainall has threatened to divorce his wife if he does not get her fortune. But Mrs Fainall denounces Mrs Marwood as her husband's mistress to Lady Wishfort, who is then advised by Mrs Marwood not to incur the publicity of a court case and subsequent public reporting of the affair in the press. Fainall makes his demands: Lady Wishfort is not to marry; Mrs Fainall is to hand over the rest of her fortune to him; the part of Millamant's fortune in Lady Wishfort's possession is to come to him through his wife because Millamant has agreed to marry Mirabell without Lady Wishfort's consent, and has refused to marry Sir Willful Witwoud. He goes off to get the legal agreements drawn up. Millamant comes in with Sir Willful, whom she says she will marry; she asks Lady Wishfort to receive Mirabell so that he can resign his contract to marry her. At Sir Willful's request she says she will suppress her resentment.

The complications multiply at high speed. Mirabell agrees to save Lady Wishfort from Fainall when he presents his demands. Foible and Mincing testify to Fainall's affair with Mrs Marwood; but this is not enough to stop him. Waitwell brings in papers which show that Mrs Fainall, before marrying Fainall, had placed her estate in trust in Mirabell's hands. This deed had been witnessed, but not read by Petulant and Witwoud; and Sir Willful had out of friendship agreed to pretend to be about to marry Millamant. The play ends with a dance, Mirabell having suggested that Mrs Fainall, now in full control of her finances, may be able to make something of her marriage. His own marriage to Millamant will now take place, with Lady Wishfort's blessing.

Detailed summaries

Title page motto

Audire est operae pretium, procedere recte
Qui maechis non vultis—   Horace, *Sat.*, 2, 1137–8
—Metuat doti deprensa—   Horace, *Sat.*, 2, 1131.

These lines from Horace can be translated thus: 'It is worth your while to listen, you do not wish things to go well for an adulteress' and 'She who is detected fears for her dowry'. The motto indicates what happens when adultery and concern for money replace respect and affection between marriage partners. The four lines at the end of the play complete the message.

The Dedication

The Dedication begins with compliments, and then goes on to say that the play's success on the stage was almost beyond Congreve's expectations, since the audience's taste has changed. Characters in contemporary comedies, he says, who are meant to be ridiculous are now such gross fools that they should be treated as objects of charity rather than despised. He himself had designed characters who are ridiculous because of their affected wit rather than natural folly, but he recognises that there is a hazard in this because members of an audience can misunderstand the author's aim. He says that he has digressed at this point because, he argues, writers who write with care and pains need to be protected and recognised. He needs the protection which will be given by the Earl of Montague's approval.

He then comments that Terence, whom he thinks the most correct writer in the world, created literature the subtleties of which his audience were incapable of appreciating; he links Terence to the Greek comic writer Menander, and through him to Theophrastus and Aristotle. Terence benefited from conversation with Scipio and Laelius, 'two of the greatest and most polite men of his age'. He attributes any merits his play may possess to the privilege of having been in the Earl's company the previous summer just before he wrote it.

Poetry (in the sense of literature) had not yet asked for the Earl's patronage, though he has aided other arts; poetry is sacred to the good and great, it can address them and they alone can protect it. He ends with a desire to distinguish the Earl as foremost among the most deserving and to pay him particular respect.

NOTES AND GLOSSARY:

Ralph, Earl of Montague: Ralph Montague (?1638–1709) was a patron of the arts and a member of the Kit-Kat club, founded in the early part of the eighteenth century, of which many leading writers were members

arraign: accuse

prefer: offer

sufficiency: self-sufficiency, confidence

censure: judgement

a Witwoud and a Truewit: Congreve's pretender to wit, Witwoud, is contrasted with Truewit, a character in Ben Jonson's (1572–1637) *Epicoene: or the Silent Woman* (1609)

Terence: Roman comic dramatist (*c*. 190–159BC)

a Scipio and a Laelius: Scipio Africanus and Gaius Laelius were distinguished Roman orators, patrons of Terence, who were members of a philosophic and literary coterie which greatly admired Greek literature

Plautus: Roman comic dramatist (?254–184BC) who translated and adapted works of the Greek new comedy. This comparison of Plautus and Terence is a commonplace of neoclassical criticism

Horace: Roman poet and satirist (65–8BC). He attacked the coarseness of Plautus in his *Ars Poetica*, the *Art of Poetry*

fable: here means plot

Menander: Greek comic dramatist (342–291BC) who greatly influenced Terence

Theophrastus: a Greek author (?372–288BC). A pupil of Aristotle, he wrote the *Characters*, sketches of thirty typical characters (for instance, the talkative person, the mean person, and so on), which were very popular in England in the seventeenth century

Aristotle: Greek philosopher (384–322BC) who greatly influenced neoclassical drama though his *Poetics*, a discussion of tragedy

your retirement: it seems that Congreve spent some of the summer at Boughton House, Montague's country residence in Northamptonshire

The Prologue

The Prologue draws a distinction between poets (whom Fortune makes and forsakes) and nature's oafs, who are looked after by Fortune as if they were cuckoo's eggs left in her nest; they absorb the care she might have given her own (the poets).

Poets are dupes; like novices in gambling, they are allowed to win a little at first, but each time they write they risk all they have already won.

Congreve has found favour before but does not argue his merits on his past record: to do so would be—here a legal metaphor is used—to risk his poetic reputation. He worked hard at the play, but tells the audience not to pity him if they think him dull. He will not resent their hissing a scene off the stage, nor attack their taste to defend his play. He thinks that the play has a good plot, new ideas, humour without farce (which may be a fault!). He then ironically remarks that satire ought not to be expected: no one would dare to correct a London which is so reformed. This time he has sought to please, not to teach. If he exposes a knave or fool by chance that does not hurt anyone in the audience since there are no knaves or fools there. The play will afford an example of an author who yields everything to the audience's judgement. So it can praise or damn the play at its own discretion.

NOTES AND GLOSSARY:
Mr Betterton: Thomas Betterton (1635–1710), though now an elderly man, was the leading actor of the period
bubbles: dupes
butter'd: flattered
Parnassus: a mountain in Greece, a few miles north of Delphi; it was sacred to the Muses
So reform'd a Town: probably a reference to Jeremy Collier's *Short View of the Profaneness and Immorality of the English Stage* (1698), though a reference to recently formed Societies for the Reformation of Manners may be intended

Act I Scene 1

Mirabell and Fainall converse after a game of cards. This introduces the facts of Fainall's being Millamant's cousin by marriage, of Mirabell's love for Millamant, of her aunt Lady Wishfort's anger against

Mirabell, of Millamant's having to gain Lady Wishfort's approval of her marriage or losing half her fortune, of Lady Wishfort's discovery that Mirabell's addresses to her were a sham to hide his love for her niece Millamant, and of Mrs Marwood's disclosure of these affairs to Lady Wishfort. Then we learn that Waitwell, Mirabell's servant, has married Lady Wishfort's servant Foible. Fainall, who has gone to see Petulant and Witwoud gambling in the next room, returns; Mirabell tells him of his feelings for Millamant. Then there is news of Sir Willful Witwoud coming to Town. We learn that he is half-brother of the Witwoud who is gambling—and paying attention to Millamant. Witwoud enters and the three discuss Sir Willful. Petulant is also discussed. When he arrives he shows his silliness and also remarks upon Mirabell's having an uncle lately come to Town, and suggests that he may come between Mirabell and Millamant.

NOTES AND GLOSSARY:

A *Chocolate house*: chocolate was served in chocolate houses as a beverage, and gentlemen often met in these fashionable places. White's Chocolate House was opened in St James's Street the year before the play was performed and was frequented by wits

humours: moods

Stoic: a person with Stoic qualities. These derive from the ancient Greek philosophy, founded by Zeno (?336–?214BC), which held that virtue and happiness come through accepting destiny and natural law

coxcomb: a foolish, conceited person, a fop—so called after the cap worn by jesters which was in the shape of a cock's comb

has a lasting passion: is very angry with you (because she has discovered that his addresses to her were 'sham' as we learn a little later in this Act)

Mrs Marwood: 'Mrs' was used at this period to designate both married and single women

vapours: depression

expecting her reply: waiting for her reply

Cabal-nights: a cabal is a clique; the five letters of the word happened to coincide with the initial letters of the names of the members of a small committee of the Privy Council in the reign of Charles II, though 'cabal' is an older word

one man ... Witwoud and Petulant: the joke is that Witwoud and Petulant are together equal to one man

ratafia:	a liqueur, generally flavoured with almonds or the kernels of cherries, peaches or apricots
dropsy:	a disease in which the body is swollen by an accumulation of liquid. Lady Wishfort 'lay in' as if in childbed
canonical hour:	from 8 am to noon were the canonical hours when marriages could take place legally
jade:	a poor horse, or a contemptuous expression for a woman
grand affair:	the marriage of Waitwell and Foible
Pancras:	St Pancras Church in London (but outside the city boundary), notorious for its irregular marriages, performed without a licence but for a fee
Duke's Place:	St James's Church in Aldgate, which had a reputation similar to that of St Pancras
shake his ears:	be lively
Dame Partlet:	from Pertelote, the hen in Geoffrey Chaucer's (?1340–1400) *Nun's Priest's Tale* in his *Canterbury Tales*. Here it is a reference to Foible
Rosamond's Pond:	a meeting place in the south-west corner of St James's Park, frequented by lovers
tender:	value
jealous:	here, suspicious
by rote:	by heart
above Forty:	a late age to undertake a tour on the continent, which was regarded as a suitable end to a young man's education
knight-errant:	a medieval knight wandering in search of adventure, here ironically applied to Sir Willful
medlar:	a brown-skinned fruit (like an apple) which only becomes edible when it begins to decay and turn pulpy
crab:	a wild apple, always sour
Monster in *The Tempest*:	Caliban, in Shakespeare's play *The Tempest*; he was made drunk by Trinculo in Act II of *The Tempest*, a version by John Dryden and William Davenant staged in 1667 and published in 1670
common place of comparisons:	a notebook used by Witwoud to jot down comparisons or similes for future use
exceptions:	difficult, liable to make objections
le Drole:	witty fellow (French *drôle*)
foreign and domestic:	the separate sections under which the news was set out in the newspapers of the time

the best woman: he means Mrs Fainall
spleen: ill temper, low spirits
bum baily: a bailiff who is always at the debtor's back
decay of parts: of intellectual ability; see 'natural parts' later in the same dialogue
positive: opinionated, certain, dogmatic
Cinnamon-water: a cordial made of powdered cinnamon, sugar, spirits and hot water
trulls: prostitutes
slip you out of: steal out of
whip: exclamation (indicating surprise)
Hackney-coach: a coach for hire
'Sbud: an oath, a contraction of 'God's blood'
persons of condition: of quality, of high rank
rub off: go, make off
Sultana Queens . . . Roxolanas: a Sultana queen is a Sultan's favourite concubine, and thus an empress: but in the seventeenth century the word meant a favourite mistress, a pun missed by Petulant, who refers to Roxolana the Turkish sultana in *The Siege of Rhodes* (1656) by Davenant
Two coheiresses his cousins and an old aunt: the cousins are Millamant and Mrs Fainall, the old aunt Lady Wishfort, Mrs Fainall's mother
catterwauling: making a noise like a cat in heat, hence a vulgar term for wooing
conventicle: a religious meeting of Non-conformists
trundle: depart, go away (to move heavily on, or as if on wheels)
paint: cosmetics
your Interpreter: he means Witwoud
an Uncle: this is part of Mirabell's plot against Lady Wishfort
snug's the word: mum's the word, silence
raillery: mockery, teasing
by thee: near, beside thee
wo't: wilt
Demme: damn me
Quaker . . . parrot: parrots proverbially repeat oaths (swear words)
fobb'd: cheated (of his marriage to Millamant and her fortune)
a humorist: a person with 'humours', or whims
the sum . . . last night: obviously Mirabell and Petulant have been talking apart from the others and now rejoin them

Quintessence:	the fifth essence, a substance of which the heavenly bodies were thought to be composed, and which was latent in all matter. Petulant is saying that he has reported the important part of what he had heard the previous night
teste a teste:	tête-à-tête, in private
the Mall:	a walk in St James's Park

Act II Scene 1

This is set in St James's Park and begins with Mrs Fainall and Mrs Marwood discussing love. The conversation turns to their dislike of men; both claim to hate Mirabell, but they are obviously fencing with one another. When Fainall and Mirabell arrive, Mrs Fainall walks apart with Mirabell while we learn that Mrs Marwood loves Fainall and suggests to him that his wife and Mirabell have an understanding. He reproaches Mrs Marwood with loving Mirabell. She threatens Fainall that she will reveal their relationship to his wife. He complains that had Mrs Marwood not told Lady Wishfort about the pretence of Mirabell's passion for her, he might have married Millamant and thus half Millamant's fortune would have come to Lady Wishfort and on her death to her daughter, his wife.

When Mrs Marwood breaks down Fainall tells her he will part from his wife. They leave and Mirabell and Mrs Fainall discuss their former love and Mirabell's plans to outwit Lady Wishfort by getting his servant Waitwell, married that morning to Foible, to court Lady Wishfort as Mirabell's pretended uncle. Mirabell will then be able to dictate terms to Lady Wishfort. At this point Millamant appears with Mincing her servant and Witwoud. After much badinage Mrs Fainall engages Witwoud in conversation and Millamant teases Mirabell, and reveals her knowledge of his plot before leaving. Mirabell then hears how Waitwell has instructed Foible how to deceive Lady Wishfort about the supposed Sir Rowland.

NOTES AND GLOSSARY:

To be free:	to be frank
you profess a libertine:	you are talking like a loose woman
Penthesilea:	Queen of the Amazons. In Greek mythology the Amazons were women warriors whom Penthesilea led to the Trojan King Priam's aid after his son Hector had been killed by the Greek warrior Achilles. Achilles wounded Penthesilea mortally and fell in love with her as she lay dying
overcome me:	taken me by surprise

Alexander: Alexander the Great, the fourth-century BC king of Macedonia, carried his conquests as far as India

oversee: overlook

insensible: lacking in sensitivity, callous

prevent (your baseness): anticipate. Mrs Marwood implies that if she is to be exposed she will make the first move and betray Fainall's infidelity to his wife

moiety: half

heart of proof: strong heart, proof against his wife's wish that he should die

asperse me: accuse me falsely

a mask: masks were fashionable at the time; they were usually made of silk or velvet

lavish: loose, licentious

servant: here, suitor

Mosca: in the last act of Ben Jonson's *Volpone or The Fox* (1607) the crafty servant Mosca insists on the exact terms of an agreement

discover the imposture betimes: reveal the deception quickly

she might . . . more privately: that she might cover up her own interest in Sir Rowland by talking about trying to bring about a match between him and Millamant

opinion . . . success: I think you are likely to be successful

green-sickness: chlorosis, a disorder formerly common in adolescent girls caused by a lack of iron; it gives a green tinge to the skin

the Fall: autumn

Here she comes . . . full sail: this passage may have been prompted by a passage in John Milton's (1608–74) *Samson Agonistes* (1671), 1.710:

> But who is this, what thing of sea or land?
> Female of sex it seems,
> That so bedecked, ornate, and gay,
> Comes this way sailing,
> Like a stately ship . . .
> With all her bravery on, and tackle trim,
> Sails filled, and streamers waving,
> Courted by all the winds that hold them play.

There is also a somewhat similar passage in Dryden's *An Evening's Love* (1668), II, where Wildblood is describing Jacintha

tenders: this can mean ships or boats attending a larger vessel, or attendants

sculler:	someone who sculls; here a boat propelled by an oar or oars
***beau-monde*:**	fashionable people, society
perukes:	wigs

Truce with your similitudes: enough of your similes (Witwoud is a tiresome utterer of similes which he collects in his commonplace book)

a hit, a hit:	compare Shakespeare's *Hamlet*, V, 2. 295: 'A hit, a very palpable hit'
O Mem:	Mincing, as her name suggests, is affected in her pronounciation; she speaks in an exaggerated, affectedly delicate way
to pin up ... hair:	to act as curling papers
tift:	tiffed, that is, titivated, arranged
Fainall:	(Mrs) Fainall
card-matches:	heavy paper matches with sulphur tips
two the:	two of the
physick:	medicine
assafoetida:	a gum resin, with a smell like garlic, from the root of *ferula asa*. It was used as a stimulant and expectorant, particularly to cure digestive disorders
a course of fools:	a course in the sense of a course of medicine
distemper:	an illness
know I:	know that I
Solomon:	The reference is to the judgement of Solomon in the Old Testament. See I Kings 3: 16–28. Tapestries often portrayed stories from the Bible
watch-light:	night-light, a candle
Turtles:	turtle-doves, lovers
Valentine's Day:	14 February, St Valentine's Day, which is associated with courtship, may derive from the Roman pagan feast of the Lupercalia, celebrated in mid-February. Two Christian Valentines seem to have been commemorated on 14 February, one a Roman priest martyred in the Flaminian Way, the other a bishop martyred in Rome
Inquietudes:	agitation, uneasiness
The lease ... the farm:	Mirabell has obviously offered to lease a farm for Waitwell and his wife if the plan succeeds
prevent her:	arrive before her
B'w'y:	God be with you
Preferment:	her marriage has given her status
attended:	waited upon

Act III Scene 1

Lady Wishfort is at her toilette, using cosmetics freely and drinking cherry brandy. Mrs Marwood arrives, to tell her that Foible, her maid, has been talking to Mirabell in the park. Lady Wishfort asks Mrs Marwood to withdraw into the closet when Foible arrives, first telling Lady Wishfort about Sir Rowland and then getting round the fact that she has been reported as talking to Mirabell by exasperating her mistress into the idea of marrying Sir Rowland to spite Mirabell.

There follow Lady Wishfort's thoughts about how she shall receive Sir Rowland. We are brought up to date with Mirabell's plan and Foible's part in it by a conversation between her and Mrs Fainall.

There is continuous movement in this act. Mrs Marwood reveals that she has heard Foible's remarks to Mrs Fainall; out of her rage at hearing that Mirabell dislikes her, she suggests to Lady Wishfort that Millamant and Sir Willful would make a good match.

Next comes a passage of raillery between Millamant and Mrs Marwood on the subject of Mirabell. A song is sung, and a conversation between the ladies and Witwoud and Petulant ensues before Millamant and her maid leave and Sir Willful Witwoud arrives. The two gallants tease Sir Willful; the half-brothers recognise each other, and Sir Willful announces his intention of travelling. Lady Wishfort enters with Fainall, welcomes her nephew and they all go to dinner—except for Fainall and Mrs Marwood who wait behind to hatch their counter-plot to Mirabell's. Mrs Marwood suggests that Fainall should tell Lady Wishfort about his wife's affair with Mirabell; she apologises for suggesting the match between Millamant and Sir Willful (Fainall has complained that her earlier disclosure to Lady Wishfort of Mirabell's plans to marry Millamant has spoiled the possibility of half Millamant's fortune going to Lady Wishfort and from her to Mrs Fainall). Fainall, however, says that he will disable Sir Willful with drink; he tells Mrs Marwood that, if the worst comes to the worst, he is already entitled to the best part of his wife's estate, and Mrs Marwood shall share in it.

NOTES AND GLOSSARY:

errant:	arrant (downright, clear)
Mopus:	a stupid person
Spanish paper:	paper impregnated with a red powder, used for reddening cheeks
changeling:	a child substituted (by fairies particularly) for another (usually in its cot), hence a simpleton
bobbins:	reels around which thread or yarn for sewing or spinning is wound

tapster: a barman

Maritornes: an Asturian chambermaid in *Don Quixote* (1605; 1615) by the Spanish author Miguel de Cervantes (1547–1616). The novel had been dramatised by Thomas D'Urfey (1653–1723) in 1694

in *dishabille*: partly or carelessly dressed (from French, *déshabillé*, undressed)

closet: a small room

Quarles: Francis Quarles (1592–1644), who wrote *Emblemes* (1635), religious meditations in rhyme

Pryn: William Prynne (1600–69), the Puritan author of *Histrio-Mastix* (1632) in which he attacked the immorality of the stage

Short View ... Stage: Rev. Jeremy Collier (1650–1726) wrote *A Short View of the Immorality and Profaneness of the English Stage* (1698) to which several dramatists, including Congreve, wrote replies (see p.6)

Bunyan's works: John Bunyan (1628–88) the tinsmith and puritan preacher, author of *The Pilgrim's Progress* (1678); his *Works* appeared in 1692

the party : the person, that is, Sir Rowland, Mirabell's supposed uncle

Miniature: a very small painting

fleers: mockery

catering: purveying, acting as an accomplice

Ods: God's

drawer: a waiter who draws ale or wine

Robin: a common name for a waiter

Lockets: a fashionable restaurant at Charing Cross

frippery: tawdry clothing (sometimes cast-off). This is an uncomplimentary reference to Lady Wishfort

Incontinently: immediately

tatterdemallion: a ragged person, a wretch

Long Lane penthouse: Long Lane (near Smithfield) was famous for its second-hand clothes shops. The penthouse implies a shed with a sloping roof

the Million Lottery: a government lottery scheme of 1694 to raise a million pounds

Birthday: Royal birthdays were lavishly celebrated by the court

Ludgate: a London prison for debtors

Angle ... mitten: prisoners dangled mittens (a kind of gloves) from Ludgate prison to beg for money from passers-by in Blackfriars below

oeconomy of face: she means she will have to make up her face again, with a consequent expense in the cosmetics used

flea'd: flayed

keep up . . . picture: live up to the portrait (the miniature which Foible has conveyed to Sir Rowland)

will a: will he

decorums: rules of proper behaviour

toilet: toilet articles

a month's mind: a liking for, an inclination

Mrs Engine: This refers to Foible's part in Mirabell's plot, which Mrs Marwood has learnt of by eavesdropping on the conversation between Foible and Mrs Fainall

My friend Fainall: Mrs Fainall

it's over: Mrs Marwood has learned of Mrs Fainall's past affair with Mirabell

horns: the traditional horns of the cuckold

without you: unless you

day of projection: the final (critical) day in an alchemist's experiment

Olio of affairs: a large number of various concerns

wou'd have fit: would have fought

doily stuff: light woollen material for summer wear

Drap-du-berry: a woollen material (of a coarse kind) from Berry, a province in central France

habit: outfit

to blind: to camouflage, disguise

burnishes: grows plumper

Rhenish-wine tea: Rhenish white wine (taken instead of tea to reduce obesity)

Comprehended in a mask: even though she was taking white wine her face could not be fitted into a mask

so particular . . . so insensible: so attentive to Millamant and so insensible to 'all the world beside'

I did not mind you: I did not have you in mind

Sybil: a prophetess. Several prophetesses of this name appear in classical mythology

to comb: to comb their wigs

Song . . . Mr Eccles: John Eccles (d. 1735) set to music many of the songs in contemporary plays

battledore: a light racket (smaller than a tennis racket) used to strike the shuttlecock in the ancient game of battledore and shuttlecock

the Ordinary: the Chaplain at Newgate Prison, who prepared prisoners for their death

setting the psalm: Alexander Pope (1688–1744) remarked in a note to his poem *The Dunciad* (1728; 1743; 1747) that it was an ancient English custom for malefactors to sing a psalm at their execution at Tyburn

Bartlemew and his Fair: St Bartholomew's Fair, held on 24 August at Smithfield

Revolution: The 'Glorious Revolution' of 1688, when William and Mary replaced James II

Oons: God's wounds

a Starling: often regarded as a stupid bird

smoke: quiz, examine with a view to mocking, making fun of, even offending

thereafter . . . meant: according to how it is meant

S'life: God's life

S'heart: God's heart

the Rekin: the Wrekin, a hill in Shropshire

Flap Dragon: a dish in which raisins were taken from blazing brandy and extinguished in the mouth. It means something worthless

scut: tail

Inns o'Court: the Inns of Court in London where law is practised and studied

Salop: Shropshire

Shrewsbury Cake: a round flat biscuit-like cake

call of Sergeants: a ceremony by which sergeants-at-law were admitted to the bar

Subpoena: a legal summons

Rat me: may God rot me

O'ds Heart: God's heart

Tale of a Cock and a Bull: a tall tale, an exaggeration

out of your time: before you had completed your legal apprenticeship

Furnival's Inn: an Inn of Court

Dawks's letter: a newsletter popular in the provinces; it began in 1696

weekly-bill: the Bill of Mortality, a report of all the deaths in and around London

the Peace: after 1688 the French king attempted to put James II back on the throne: the war (1689–97) which resulted was ended by the Treaty of Ryswick. Four years later the War of the Spanish Succession began

at all adventures: whatever happens

shill I, shall I: shilly-shally, dither

rallier:	one given to good-humoured, fashionable ridicule
to chuse:	as they like
satyr:	a mythological creature, half man half goat, with budding horns
citizen's child:	citizen's wives were frequently represented (in the comedies of the period) as having liaisons with young gallants; thus, it means a cuckold's child
fond:	foolish

furnish'd . . . Deputy-Lieutenant's hall: decorated with antlers

Cap of Maintenance: part of the regalia carried before the sovereign at the state opening of Parliament: in heraldry it is a cap with two points like horns behind. There is a pun on the word maintenance, as Mrs Marwood is suggesting that Fainall, because he now knows of his wife's adultery, may be able to blackmail Lady Wishfort

can away with :	put up with
Pam:	the knave of clubs, the highest trump card in the game of loo; Mrs Fainall hence has potential mastery of the situation
composition:	agreement
has an appearance:	has possibilities
like a Dane:	the Danes were regarded as very heavy drinkers
set his hand at:	get him to drink
the branches:	cuckold's horns

knows some passages: knows of Mrs Marwood's affair with Fainall

turn my wife to grass: as a farmer would put an old animal out to graze

---

Act IV Scene 1

The scene is the same. Lady Wishfort considers how she will receive Sir Rowland; she tells Foible to call Millamant downstairs and she will herself send Sir Willful to her, to propose to her. But Foible waits to tell Millamant, who comes in with Mrs Fainall, that Mirabell wants to see her. Sir Willful arrives, and Mrs Fainall leaves, locking the door after her. Sir Willful exhibits his lack of Town manners, and leaves by another door. Mirabell comes in and there ensues the famous discussion between him and Millamant in which they agree how they will conduct themselves in marriage. Millamant agrees to marry him. Mrs Fainall returns to warn Mirabell to slip away as her mother is returning, having had to leave Sir Rowland to deal with Sir Willful who is drunk—as is Witwoud who enters, to be followed by Petulant, also drunk. Then Sir Willful enters with Lady Wishfort. He is very drunk, an excuse for Millamant and Mrs Fainall to leave.

Lady Wishfort sends him off when she hears Sir Rowland is impatient, and she and Sir Rowland agree to marry. She leaves to receive a letter, and returns with it to discover it is an anonymous denunciation of Sir Rowland as a rascal and a cheat. The supposed Sir Rowland at the prompting of Foible pretends the letter is from Mirabell, and tells Lady Wishfort he will bring her a black box 'which contains the writings' of his whole estate.

NOTES AND GLOSSARY:

pulvill'd: perfumed

levee: rising

There never . . . to be curs'd: the opening lines of an untitled poem by Sir John Suckling (1609–42)

Thyrsis . . . train: the first line of a poem by Edmund Waller (1606–87) entitled 'The Story of Phoebus and Daphne, applied'. Other lines of this poem are quoted later by Millamant and Mirabell

undergo: put up with

I prithee . . . slight toy: the first two lines of a 'Song', by Suckling. The rest of the poem's first stanza, three lines, are quoted by Millamant in her next two speeches

Anan?:   Pardon?

Gothick: to the neoclassical taste of the Restoration and early eighteenth century Gothic art seemed crude and inelegant

lingo: language which is difficult to understand

fetch a walk: take a walk

fought: fetched, or taken: 'fought' is a provincial form ('sought' might be the correct reading here but 'fought' seems better as more comic and suiting Sir Willful's country speech)

l'etourdie: a stupid, or thoughtless person

spare . . . speed: if you don't speak you won't get on, a proverbial expression

all a case: it doesn't matter

Like Phoebus . . . Boy: the third line of Waller's poem 'The Story of Phoebus and Daphne, applied'

Like Daphne . . . Coy: the fourth line of Waller's poem; Mirabell completes the couplet just begun by Millamant

curious: difficult, complex

instant: pressing

pragmatical: matter-of-fact

douceurs: pleasures

Someils du Matin: day-dreams

chariot: four-wheeled light carriage

interrogatories: questions
Imprimis: first of all
Covenant: decree
wheadle: procure secretly
to the play in a mask: only loose women wore masks at the theatre
hog's bones . . . cat: all these were then used in the making of cosmetics
gentlewomen . . . Court: some topical reference, the meaning of which is not known
atlasses: a silk-satin manufactured in the East
crooked-billet: a bent stick
anniseed . . . ratafia: all these drinks were based on brandy, with various flavours
clary: a drink made with wine and honey, with ginger and pepper to flavour it
dormitives: sedatives
unsiz'd camlet: size is used to stiffen textiles; camlet was originally a costly material from the East, of silk and camel's hair. After the sixteenth century it began to be made of angora goats' hair. The word came to mean also a garment made of cheap material. The image is of a garment being fitted by having pieces let into it, probably after shrinking
Noli prosequi: a legal term: the case is stopped as the plaintiff does not wish to continue the prosecution
whim it: spin
Folios: books with the leaves made of sheets of paper folded in half
Decimo sexto: a book half the size of an octavo volume, in which each leaf is a sixteenth of a full sheet of paper
Lacedemonian: spartan; the Spartans were sparing in words (the word 'laconic' comes from Laconia, the district of Greece in which Sparta was situated)
Baldwin: the ass in a medieval tale, *Reynard the Fox*
Gemini: a pair of twins
rantipole: wild
Borachio: a drunkard (from the Spanish word for wine bag)
grutch: grudge
In vino veritas: (*Latin*) there is truth in wine
pimple: a boon companion
tallow chandler: a person who makes, sells or deals in candles; here a maker of them
believe not . . . grape: Mohammedans do not drink wine
Mufti: a Mohammedan priest and an expert in religious law

Sultan:	the sovereign of a Muslim country, especially of the former Ottoman empire
Sophy:	the surname of the ruling dynasty in Persia [Sufi] (from *c.* 1500 to 1736); the word was used as a title of the Persian ruler
tumbril:	dung cart
bastinado'd:	beaten (probably on the soles of the feet)
shake-bag:	a term used in cock-fighting, a very game, sporting cock
bite your cheek:	kiss your cheek
Salopian:	native of Shropshire
thy pig:	the pig was associated with St Anthony (Tantony: St Anthony). The smallest pig in a litter was sometimes called Tantony. Here, then, the word is presumably applied to Witwoud in that sense
Year of Jubilee:	the first Jubilee year was instituted by Pope Boniface VIII in 1300; he intended that a jubilee should be celebrated every hundred years, but Pope Paul II decided twenty-five years should be the interval. There was a jubilee in 1700, the year *The Way of the World* was first performed
tenter:	on the tenterhook, in painful suspense
save-all:	a device to ensure that all of a candle in a candlestick will be completely burned
iteration:	repetition
camphire:	camphor, which was supposed to reduce sexual desire
chairman ... dog-days:	I'd rather carry a sedan chair in the hottest part of the summer
suborn'd:	bribed
his date is short:	his days are numbered
*arrant knight ... arrant knave***:**	arrant (meaning errant, wandering) can be used in different ways. The knight here, is 'genuine'; the knave is an 'utter' knave, an 'unmitigated' knave

Act V Scene 1

Lady Wishfort comes in, furiously abusing Foible for her part in the plot to marry her to the supposed Sir Rowland. Foible, trying to mitigate her mistress's anger, tells her that Waitwell could not have married her anyway as he had already married Foible herself. This further enrages Lady Wishfort who goes off for a constable, intending that Foible shall join Waitwell in prison, Fainall having had him arrested. Mrs Fainall then comforts Foible with the news that Mirabell has gone to get Waitwell out of prison; in turn Foible tells her that though her former affair with Mirabell is known, her husband has been involved with Mrs Marwood.

Next the tension is increased by Mincing telling them Waitwell has been set free, that Fainall has upset Lady Wishfort, that Mirabell and Millamant have sent for Sir Willful, and that it looks as if Millamant will marry him to save her fortune from Lady Wishfort. Mincing and Foible leave and Lady Wishfort returns, thanking Mrs Marwood for having originally told her Mirabell was false and then that Sir Rowland was an impostor, and now for interceding with her son-in-law. Mrs Fainall denounces Mrs Marwood to her mother and defends herself before leaving. Lady Wishfort is swayed by this and says that Fainall will have to prove his wife's disloyalty; at this Mrs Marwood tells her of the unpleasantness that will ensue if the matter comes to court, or, worse, reaches the press. Lady Wishfort then thinks she will settle on Fainall's terms if he hushes up the matter. These are severe: she is not to marry unless the husband is of his choice; the remainder of his wife's fortune is to be settled on him and he will give her what he thinks fit for her maintenance; he is to be endowed with Millamant's six thousand pounds because she has contracted herself without Lady Wishfort's permission to Mirabell, and has refused Sir Willful. He leaves to get the legal documents drawn up.

Millamant and Sir Willful come in and say that they will marry, but that Mirabell must resign his contract in Lady Wishfort's presence. He and Sir Willful are going abroad together. Lady Wishfort forgives him, but when Fainall returns he believes neither in the marriage plans nor in Mirabell's abandonment of Millamant. When Mirabell says he can save Mrs Fainall from ruin, Lady Wishfort says she will agree to his marrying Millamant.

Foible then enters with Mrs Fainall and Mincing: the plot of Fainall and Mrs Marwood is made clear by the two women servants, but Fainall is not deterred. It is the entry of Waitwell with the black box which changes everything. Petulant and Witwoud come in to testify they were witnesses to a document: in this Mrs Fainall, before her marriage, had conveyed her estate in trust to Mirabell, and as this deed antedated her marriage Fainall's claim upon her money is invalid. It is then revealed that Sir Willful had merely been helping Mirabell and Millamant, Lady Wishfort agrees to their marriage and Mirabell expresses the hope that through the Deed of Trust Fainall and Mrs Fainall may yet make their marriage work.

NOTES AND GLOSSARY:

chafing-dish: a vessel for heating anything placed on it

Traver's rag: traverse rag, a curtain drawn across a room as a screen

flaunting ... packthread: dangling in a gaudy way on stout twine

bulk: stall

dead: continuous

frisoneer-gorget: a portion of cloth covering a woman's neck and breast. *Frisoneer* is probably from *frison*, *frieze*; a coarse woollen material

Colberteen: cheap French lace, made by M. Colbert, Superintendent of the French King's Manufacturers

upon ... clergy: forced to plead benefit of clergy. Up to 1827 a felon on his first conviction could claim exemption from the sentence for some offences provided he could read

meddle or make: interfere, a proverbial expression

Abigails and Andrews: names given to maids and men servants

Philander: the lover in Ariosto's (1474–1533) *Orlando Furioso* (1532) and Beaumont (1584–1616) and Fletcher's (1579–1625) *The Laws of Candy* (1647)

Dukes-Place: see note, p.17; she means, marry you in a hurry

Bridewell: a house of correction, a prison for women

sheep by groves and purling streams ... shepherdesses: common images in pastoral poetry

naught: immoral, naughty

sophisticated: false

temper: moderation

Counter: a token, an imitation coin

composition: restitution

babies: dolls

made a shift: contrived

going in her fifteen: about to reach her fifteenth birthday

O Yes: *Oyez* is the Old French for 'Hear Ye', shouted by a court officer in order to command silence at the beginning of a court case

quoif: a lawyer's white cap

Cantharides: Spanish fly, an aphrodisiac; it was also used as a diuretic and, externally, as a blistering agent

cow-itch: cowage, a stinging plant

the Temple: the Inner or Middle Temple Inns of Court

prentices ... conventicle: apprentices had often to keep notes of sermons for their masters

Commons: a dining hall or the main meal served there

drawers: barmen, tapsters

flounder-man: a seller of flounders, flat fish (a reference to an actual character of the time)

grey-pease: the grey field pea, *pisum arvense* (as opposed to the garden pea, *pisum sativum*)

overseen: overlooked

Muscovite husband: a Russian husband; they were notorious wife-beaters

Czarish ... retinue: the Czar Peter the Great visited England in 1697

non-Compos: (*Latin*) *non compos mentis*, not in command of himself; in this case, drunk

Instrument is drawing: the legal agreement is being made up

ballance: weigh up, ponder

her year: her year's mourning (the normal period) for her first husband

with a witness: and no mistake

at this rebel rate: probably a reference to the sequestration of Royalist property after the Civil War

Egyptian plagues: see the Bible, Exodus 7–12

Gorgon: one of the three mythological sisters, Stheno, Euryale and Medusa, who could turn to stone anyone on whom they turned their eyes

Pylades and Orestes: in Greek legend Pylades was the faithful friend of Orestes, the son of Agamemnon and Clytemnestra. After Clytemnestra and her lover Aegisthus killed Agamemnon on his return from Troy, Pylades helped Orestes to avenge his father's death by killing Clytemnestra and Aegisthus. Later Pylades married Electra, Orestes's sister

An: if

O' the Quorum: Justice of the Peace

mouth-glew: glue activated by being moistened by the tongue; hence figuratively, 'glue' made of words. Sir Willful is saying that no marriage contract was drawn up on paper

Papers of Concern: important papers

fox: a kind of sword

Ram vellam: parchment

Mittimus: a warrant

tailor's measure: often made of parchment at this time

respite: control

Beefeater: a guard in the Tower of London

bear-garden: bear-baiting was popular, and the places where it was carried on were noisy and rowdy

Messalina's poems:	Mincing means a volume of miscellaneous poems, a miscellany. Messalina, wife of the Roman Emperor Claudius, was known for her promiscuity and greed
groat:	a coin worth four pence
who's hand's out:	who is making a mistake (a reference to Fainall); the image is from a card game
elder:	earlier
off or on:	one way or the other

The Epilogue

Congreve is thinking how the play will be pulled to pieces after the epilogue, but, he says, before you condemn it, consider how hard it would be to please all the audience. There are some critics who come determined not to be pleased, and anyone who pleases them must have more than human skill. All bad poets will be hostile, and it is known how greatly their numbers have increased. He has seen very many of them in the pit judging the play, though their only pretence for judging is that they themselves have been condemned for lack of wit. Since then, taught by their own mistakes, they have become fault-finders with the plays of others. There are others, whose malice he would like to arrest, who pretend to know there are real persons drawn in the characters of the play; they thus turn satire into libel. He hopes such malicious fops will find they are themselves shown up as fools—if they are vain enough to think their foolishness could support dramatic representation and be entertaining. Sensible, intelligent people know satire does not stoop so low as to portray a fop. When painters paint a simple portrait of a fine face, they blend in different features from other beauties, and poets similarly expose whole assemblies of coquettes and beaux in one play.

NOTES AND GLOSSARY:

Poets:	dramatists in the pit: dramatists received free seats in the pit
glosses:	interpretation
abstracted:	particular

Commentary

The plot

The plot of *The Way of the World* is complicated, and becomes more so as the play progresses. Indeed Congreve thought, as he tells us in the Dedication, that contemporary audiences were unappreciative, unable to grasp—and value—the wit he had so brilliantly created for them. He blamed the play's relative unpopularity when it was first staged on the change in the taste of the audience, a liking for fools and farce rather than wits and satiric comedy; but it could be argued that the intricacies of the plot make the play hard to follow, especially if it is played fast on the stage (as it should be) in order to keep the repartee crisp. The close relationships between the characters of the play, whose past histories are not known as they usually are in mythical or historical plays, have to be explained. The fact that Mrs Fainall was Mirabell's mistress, and was married off to Fainall to avoid a scandal when she suspected she was pregnant, is an example of how Congreve included events that took place before the play's action. He does this to explain the present feelings and motivations of the characters as well as the seeming discrepancies between the public and private relationships. This technique adds subtleties to the play's action and characterisation.

Congreve, however, is not always easy to follow. We learn that Mirabell has enraged Lady Wishfort by pretending to be in love with her, and this adds to the dramatic content of the comedy by making his task of winning her approval of his marriage to Millamant all the more difficult. Congreve uses Mirabell's confession (in Act I) as a joke, a means of ridiculing older women, but his action is still unexplained. Why should Mirabell, who plans his behaviour so cunningly, act the lover to Lady Wishfort? If he really wants to marry Millamant, which he does, this deception will have to come out and obviously will not help him to win over Lady Wishfort and gain her agreement to both the marriage and to Millamant's having all her fortune at her own disposal.

Again, what are we to make of the fact that Mirabell tells Mrs Fainall that he knew Fainall was a designing lover and yet had arranged her marriage to him? Does this imply that Fainall was false to Mrs Marwood? When Fainall and Mrs Marwood argue together in the Park the one clear thing about Fainall seems to be his devotion to her. It is, indeed, hard to pinpoint Congreve's meaning. What do we make of Mrs Marwood? She is obviously an expert liar, but it is difficult sometimes to know if she is lying or telling the truth. This poses different problems, greater ones than merely recognising discrepancies, such as that between Mrs Marwood's original statement that she will send Lady Wishfort a letter 'from an unknown hand' and Foible's instant recognition of her writing when the letter is delivered—'By Heav'n Mrs Marwood's, I know it.' Perhaps Mrs Marwood meant that she would not sign the letter; perhaps she could not find anyone else to write it; perhaps she could not disguise her writing; perhaps Foible's realisation of who had written the letter is proof of her own sharp intelligence. Or, most likely, Congreve may not have noticed the discrepancy.

These points (and others like them which could also be made) should not detract from an appreciation of the construction of the plot which is carefully balanced. The loveless marriage of the Fainalls is set against that which Mirabell and Millamant hope to base upon mutual respect and trust. The would-be wits, Witwoud and Petulant, are to be measured against the true wits, Mirabell and Fainall: but, within these categories of would-be wits and true wits, Witwoud and Petulant are different, as are Mirabell and Fainall. Fainall, for instance, is cynical about adultery; he has not allowed for the generosity of others, whereas Mirabell stands for an improvement in personal relationships. There are contrasts between town and country, Sir Wilful standing for the country and speaking in plain country fashion. There is tension between youth and age, for the plot balances the power of the old, in Lady Wishfort, against the wishes of the young, notably Mirabell and Millamant. Differing points of view are thus expressed; and change can come about. Mirabell is a reformed rake who wants to construct in his marriage a lasting union, whereas Fainall is destructive in his attitude, and solely motivated by personal desires.

Construction: the unities

Congreve was obviously influenced by neoclassical theories about drama; to achieve the regularity of form praised by neoclassical critics meant keeping to the three unities, principles of dramatic composition based upon Aristotle's *Poetics*, as expanded by sixteenth-century Italian and seventeenth-century French critics. These were that a play should consist of one main action, occurring at one time (not longer than the play takes to perform on the stage), and in one place. The three unities were often modified—the time limit could extend to twenty-four hours, for example, and the place to one house or town rather than one room or street.

Congreve's action revolves around whether Mirabell or Fainall will succeed in their plans to manipulate Lady Wishfort. The action takes place within a day, as is made clear in the text. And it takes place in London, the first act being set in a chocolate house, the second in St James's Park and the three subsequent acts in Lady Wishfort's house.

Beyond possessing a necessary degree of fashionable elegance, neither the settings nor the clothes worn by the characters are particularly significant. Congreve was portraying fashionable life in the London of his day.

Materialism

The Way of the World is a very materialistic play. There is no mysticism, no innocence, here. Lack of knowledge implies stupidity; for instance, Lady Wishfort's failure to understand the true nature of people's motives leads to her being easily and frequently manipulated by many of the other characters such as Mirabell and the servants Foible and Waitwell and, later, by Sir Willful and Millamant as well as by Mrs Marwood and Fainall.

Congreve is dealing with material elements of life: money, sex, and power. His setting is metropolitan: his city characters despise those from the country, the servant Peg and Sir Willful Witwoud, whose rural background implies rustic buffoonery (though he is actually honest and kindly).

Sir Willful comes from the Wrekin in Shropshire: viewed from London this area is obviously regarded as an uncouth place, a provincial backwater, but as the tide turned against sophisticated urban comedy this same area was chosen by George Farquhar as the scene of the action of his successful comedy *The Recruiting Officer* in which country people are allowed their own merits (see p.8). But when Fainall uses the image of 'herding' he does it to imply contempt. Lady Wishfort's vision of escaping from London as a shepherdess to a pastoral paradise, complete with purling streams, is presented as a pathetic attempt to avoid pressing problems.

The fashionable world of the Town, of London, was based upon materialistic views. It does not occur to Mirabell that he should marry Millamant without her whole fortune of twelve thousand pounds. Fainall married his wife for her money, and is ready to divorce her to get more money, and when Mirabell's plot succeeds, Mirabell implies that the Fainall marriage will be maintained socially because Fainall will not be able to withstand the lure of his wife's cash.

Women have power when they have money to bestow: that, for instance, is why Lady Wishfort is the target of two plots, Mirabell's and Fainall's. Millamant has a fortune and so she attracts admirers.

But women have also the power of sexual attractiveness. Lady Wishfort's tragedy is that she has lost this with age, but not her desire for what she calls 'iteration of nuptials'. This, implied by her name, is what make her vulnerable to the supposed Sir Rowland's advances (as she, no doubt, earlier encouraged Mirabell's approaches). Mrs Fainall attracted Mirabell when she was a widow; Mrs Marwood attracts Fainall who is prepared to spend his wife's money on her. There is, however, a limitation in all this in that husbands control their wives' finances by law (the Married Women's Property Act which gave women control of their own money was not passed until 1882!).

The negative aspects of the power of sexual attraction and money were obviously age and poverty (Lady Wishfort's threats to Foible are very real). Equally, however, a loss of social power was suffered by those whose reputations were damaged by scandal. This is why Lady Wishfort is so affected when Mrs Marwood blackmails her by conjuring up the effects of a trial and the harm that the subsequent scandal could do. Earlier Mirabell married off Arabella to Fainall to avoid scandal. And even the cynical rake Fainall tried to stop Mrs Marwood's intimate disclosures because he feared the effect of gossip. Power included projecting the right image of oneself publicly, an image which was socially acceptable, within the norms of the then fashionable world.

Realism

The Way of the World presents life persuasively with all its fluctuations, its changing circumstances. This is a world without absolute values, with ambiguous moral judgements, with emotional attachments overlapping, shifting, waxing and waning. Congreve shows us that even the attraction Mirabell and Millamant feel for each other is mutable. His lovers, despite all their sophistication, are overwhelmed by powerful feelings. Mirabell calculatingly reckons up Millamant's faults, but this attempted objectivity merely makes him more her slave. Logic does not rule; Mirabell is obsessed, fearing—when he gains her—that he loves her too much. Millamant similarly barters her freedom away, cherishing means of securing her privacy and self-respect, but she is forced ultimately to gamble with 'violent' passion. She chooses marriage, sharply aware that if Mirabell should prove false she will be 'a lost thing'. And while Congreve certainly suggests that they are approaching marriage in a way that should secure their happiness, this is a comedy where nothing is certain. There is a stimulating vitality in the play's uncertainty; it has the energy of life itself.

Wit and wisdom

Wit can be defined as an ability to describe ideas in unusual and arresting terms, to make pithy comments; but in order to make these comments perception is needed. Thus while Congreve talks of wit in terms of verbal sparring, of cynical or frivolous talk—no doubt the kind of conversational exchanges he admired at his patron's house and elsewhere in fashionable society, and in the coffee and chocolate houses—he also implies a deeper understanding of life and the way it works. Just as the 'fool' is often traditionally the wisest person on stage, so the wit, or humorist, in Congreve's play is a joker who knows more about what is actually going on than any of the other characters. And Congreve, talking about the way audiences reacted to his play, made the same distinction between the people who watched his work on the stage: they, too, were wits and would-be wits. The real wits appreciate the subtle distinctions between each character's brand of wit, differentiating, in a swift give-and-take of 'funny' lines, between those which were really astute, relatively astute, or sporadically astute.

Thus, in the inventive exchanges between Mirabell and Millamant, Congreve presents the marriage of true and sparkling minds, whereas exchanges between these characters and Witwoud (whose mind is either forgetful or clogged with irrelevancies) show the latter at a disadvantage. Fainall implies that it takes both Petulant and Witwoud together to make a complete man: Witwoud seems the wittier of the two but he is so anxious to gain the reputation of a wit that—while he can expose Mincing's affectation—he idiotically interprets Petulant's rudeness and bad language as 'Fire and Life'.

Humour

The ironic tone of the play is clear from the start when Congreve refers in his Prologue to 'so Reform'd a Town'. Disapproval of sexual experimentation was again coming into fashion, and Congreve—writing with the freedom of the Restoration—found it hypocritical. When the Restoration dramatists first explored sexual innuendo, intrigue and 'liberal' attitudes, they wrote with all the gusto which supersedes suppression. By Congreve's time, however, this energy was evaporating and the tide was beginning to turn again towards a more rigidly moralistic approach. Congreve's amoral wit, however, is designed to shock the puritan. Witwoud, for example, apologises to Fainall for asking after his wife when Fainall is, after all, a man of pleasure and of the Town. Domestic pleasures were out of place, not to say threatened, in the Restoration theatre which thrived on adultery and cynicism. If a lack of appreciation made this Congreve's last play, then the play itself offers a permanent gibe at its limited critics: surely it is significant that the sex-starved Lady Wishfort is the only character with a careful display of moralistic books.

Congreve makes sophisticated use of traditional sexual material. The idea of the battle of the sexes is frequently presented, each side astutely criticising the other's combined cruelties and vanities. Mrs Marwood and Mrs Fainall discuss the ironies of pursuit and retreat, while Millamant's and Mirabell's affair highlights the vulnerability of legalised love, as Millamant fears that marriage may kill passion. Congreve exploits the humorous ups and downs of courtship, the barbed emotional exchanges in an unhappy marriage (the Fainalls') and the ironies of the classic triangle in the relationship between Fainall, his wife, and his mistress. The comic potential of the frustrated cuckold is seen in Fainall (when he learns of Mrs Fainall's past) and of the bashful lover in the tongue-tied Sir Willful (who, when drunk, bursts into song and seeks the more readily available and presumably less fastidious company of the maids). Similarly, Congreve satirises the way Waitwell's enjoyment of his new bride is subdued by his encounter with Lady Wishfort. The main power struggle occurs when the position of an old person with authority (Lady Wishfort) is challenged by two young lovers, who then reunite the family. Congreve adds to this basic drama by making Lady Wishfort personify another stock victim, the older woman infatuated with a youthful upstart; her final humiliation coming when—all her airs and graces forgotten—she asks if she cannot have a man for medical reasons.

Another stock device, deftly treated, is the discrepancy between town and country thinking. Thus the simple Peg, Lady Wishfort's maid, does not realise that her employer wants to drink copiously but hide the evidence. And Sir Willful is surprised to find lunch served in what, by country standards, would have been called the afternoon. His lack of sophistication, or hypocrisy, is put down, in part, to a lack of education: he has reached middle age without the experience of European travel, then considered the highlight of a gentleman's education. Congreve also parodies Lady Wishfort's foolishness in keeping her daughter in deliberate ignorance of men and worldly affairs.

Congreve does not rely very heavily on visual humour. There are examples of ironic concealment, such as when Peg (having already got into trouble for producing such a tiny cup) has quickly to conceal the bottle under the table, or when Mrs Marwood hears her enemies discussing her while she is hiding in Lady Wishfort's closet. There are also examples of visual humour, such as the implied differences between Sir Willful's travel-stained clothing and his half-brother Antony Witwoud's fanciful town costume.

Similarly, Sir Willful's drunken episode, or the scene of Lady Wishfort at her toilette, conjure up picturesque images. But Congreve's humour is essentially verbal. Characters react to social situations, their conversations making us laugh because there are so many strands of irony at work.

Congreve's style

Congreve, who praised conversation in his dedication, had the gift of making his dialogue appear deceptively natural. It is, in fact, both elegant and polished. Its free and easy flow contains a great variety of speech, from Witwoud's absurd similes to Lady Wishfort's long strings of vivacious, picturesque images and, in contrast, Petulant's brief, simplistic remarks. Mirabell is arresting, Millamant gracefully playful, Marwood full of mocking bitterness and all are equally convincing, recapturing perhaps the spontaneity that Congreve admired so much in the Earl of Montague and in his other friends, such as the Irish author Jonathan Swift, a master of deceptively casual, biting rhetoric.

Congreve is intrigued by, and parodies, all forms of language—including the drunken non-communication of Petulant and Willful, which he likens to the spluttering of two roasting apples. Sir Willful's singing episode with Petulant and Witwoud shows the more relaxed side of a previously bashful lover. Congreve also makes fun of women's foibles. Mirabell, for example, teases Millamant when he says that there are two things women cannot do without in life: 'To your Lover you owe the pleasure of leaving yourselves prais'd; and to an Eccho the pleasure of hearing yourselves talk.' Witwoud adds that he knows a lady who speaks so much that an echo would have to wait until she died in order to catch up with her. He obviously is describing Lady Wishfort, whose love of gossip rebounds on her when she becomes the victim of two plots (Mirabell's and Marwood's), both of which depend on her fear of scandal attaching itself to either herself or her daughter.

Talk, then, is not just a frivolous but a powerful weapon in a play which depends on it to carry not only ideas, but drama. Think how few dramatic moments are physical ones in Congreve's play. For example, when Fainall grabs Mrs Marwood's hands it is not his gesture but her response to it, her remark that she would happily lose them to be free, that stays in our memory.

Congreve's written word is varied, in epigram, speech and song; he also enjoys parody—for example, Sir Willful's account of how Witwoud when first in Town wrote natural letters but later foppish, more pretentious ones, and Millamant's use of poems as curling papers.

Congreve was obviously interested in the difference between what people said and did publicly and what they actually felt: a discrepancy often marked by a tell-tale blush or loss of colour, as Mrs Marwood and Mrs Fainall point out. He was also interested in secrecy and concealment and realised their dramatic effectiveness: see, for instance, his use of the closet, the attic, the backstairs, the black box, masks and disguise. His most telling images often exploit actual material surfaces —'Fools are such Drap-du-berry things', says Millamant, cruelly equating them with dull, hard-wearing cloth. Lady Wishfort's picture must sit to her, says Foible archly, reversing the usual order as she paints her mistress with enough make-up to camouflage the 'old peel'd wall'. The same point is made, in more courtly fashion, by Sir Willful, who is reminded of the wrinkled skin of a cream cheese, and reassures Mirabell that Lady Wishfort cannot laugh as her face is 'none of her own'.

Much imagery derives from the law and from gambling, though there is also some religious imagery. The villainess, Mrs Marwood, is referred to as a devil; Mrs Fainall is a pattern of generosity; Mirabell is a prodigal, and Foible a penitent; Lady Wishfort is urged, as she is a Christian, to pardon and forgive—in the best comic tradition. It is possible to see contemporary political innuendo in the reference to Lady Wishfort's cabal.

Literature itself is one of the main sources of inspiration in this play which gracefully reflects its author's erudition and wit. It is amusing, for example, that Lady Wishfort indicates that she has read Cervantes's novel *Don Quixote* but shows no such knowledge of the moralistic books displayed in her closet. Congreve mentions, in his Dedication, that he is working in the classical tradition established in ancient Greece and Rome. He introduces this comedy with Latin quotations, and makes many varied references to other literary works, from Chaucer's time to his own. The name Witwoud, for example, alludes to the name 'Truewit' in a play by Ben Jonson, while Mirabell makes a direct reference to Jonson when he says he has made Waitwell marry so that he cannot outwit him, as Volpone's servant did in *The Fox*. His talk of 'plain dealing' recalls the cynicism of William Wycherley's (?1640–1716) *The Plain Dealer* (1676), another Restoration comedy, while his contemporaries would probably have found echoes of his friend and mentor John Dryden's Caliban in Sir Willful, and recognised Milton's description of Delilah and Dryden's picture of Cleopatra as a ship as the inspirations for Congreve's own image of Millamant bearing down like a ship in full sail.

Millamant criticises Petulant for his illiteracy, and wonders that any ill-educated man dares to make love to her. She is expressing Congreve's intellectual snobbism: it is significant that while poor rustic Sir Willful (who cannot even speak the polite language of the day, French) is unable to understand her when she quotes poetry, Fainall, a clever rake and man-about-town, recognises what she is quoting; but Mirabell, her intellectual equal, manages to cap her quotation with one to his own advantage, thus beginning the successful conclusion to his courtship.

Sir John Suckling (1609–42), one of the poets Millamant quotes, provides Congreve with a joke. She lets Sir Willful (who has become middle-aged without maturing) confuse this name with the idea of a youth or stripling. Suckling is also a term for a young pig, and Sir Willful later, when drunk, calls himself Tantony, or Pig. There is a host of such jokes all based on misunderstandings. Thus Peg, the country maid, mistakes 'Red' rouge for red alcohol, thinking it must mean the cherry brandy or the ratafia. Mincing, too, wants to discredit an oath sworn not on a Bible but a book of miscellaneous poetry but says 'Messalina's poems', referring to a most promiscuous Roman empress.

There is also an ironic double entendre to be noted in the speech of the main characters. The word 'friend' is frequently employed: Mirabell uses it as a synonym for 'lover' when he first alerts us to the hypocrisy of Fainall's involvement with his wife's friend, Mrs Marwood; the idea of the latter as the 'friend' or good genius of Lady Wishfort, the woman she is bent on destroying, is equally ironic. Waitwell and his wife play on the double meaning of 'knight errant' ('errant' meaning either wandering in search of adventure or erring from the right course or standards) when the former takes the part of Sir Rowland, while Mirabell's cynical repetition of Fainall's self-excusing phrase 'the way of the world' shows that he has beaten Fainall at his own game.

The names of the characters suit their natures. Fainall, feign all, provides a clue to Fainall's character, just as the name of his wife's late husband—Languish—suggests an ineffectual personality. The Wishforts' composite surname suggests that they are people with strong desires or wishes. The French word 'fort' combined with 'for't' = for it (like the French *amant*, lover, at the end of Millamant's name) adds to the meaning of the complete name, just as 'mar' in Marwood means to spoil, and indicates that her character is that of a spoiler, one who ruins things. But Congreve can also be more direct—Waitwell for example, is absolutely reliable. This juxtaposition of the direct and the subtle is one of Congreve's ways of being humourous, as, for example, when he moves from a fulsome description of the three mysterious ladies who have come to call on Petulant to Witwoud's abrupt explanation that they are, in fact, three trollops. Congreve's metaphors are striking, as, for instance, when Waitwell tells his wife that Lady Wishfort is the Antidote to Desire. So, too, is his use of question-and-answer technique as a means of imparting information—see how Congreve uses the original conversation between Mirabell and Fainall

to reveal major facts, including past events, which the audience needs to understand in order to follow the complexities of his plot. As the play progresses the author relies on his audience to keep their wits about them. An obvious question demands a factual answer, but in Congreve's play both questions and answers can be equally suspect, as so many of his characters use them both as verbal tricks for camouflage and attack, joyfully disconcerting, deliberately misinforming.

The play's conclusion

The Way of the World is a traditional love story in that the hero woos and wins the heroine. And, although these two do build up mutual trust, there is dissatisfaction amongst many of the surrounding characters which creates a subtle element of doubt about everything. It is highly probable that the hero and heroine will live happily ever after, continuing to help to protect Lady Wishfort and her daughter; but Congreve's world is treacherous and uncertain. Few people change. Mrs Fainall is tied to an unpleasant husband, even if she avoids a public scandal. Mrs Marwood leaves the stage and evil is averted, in the best comic tradition; but there is nothing to stop her being cruel again in the future. Fainall does not appear to have learnt anything from his experiences. Lady Wishfort, Witwoud, Petulant and Sir Willful remain as self-deluding as ever, so, although Congreve avoids obvious punishments—apart from feelings of resentment and humiliation—he also avoids a general development and growth of love amongst his characters. His treatment of love is limited. Seen, however, in the context of the Restoration theatre his condemnation of a marriage of convenience, based on self-interest and financial interest, and indeed on an all-round cynicism, is most unusual. Compare, say, the earlier plays of John Dryden, George Etherege, William Wycherley, Edward Ravenscroft and Aphra Behn. Congreve's optimism is only restricted when taken out of the context of the seventeenth-century comedy of manners.

The characters

Fainall

Fainall is a cynic. Like Mirabell he is a man-about-town, but as the drama progresses we observe that he seems to have developed less of a sense of good and evil than Mirabell. See, for example, his reaction to the news that Mrs Fainall had been, before her marriage to him, Mirabell's mistress. In Fainall's mind falsehood is to be expected; since deceit constitutes 'the way of the world' it is simply a question of who fools whom first. Fainall despises marriage: to him it is a farce, an empty form of legal imprisonment. This negative view of life—Fainall's own lack of kindness and responsibility—is reflected in the other characters' negative reactions to him. It is significant that he and his partner in ill intent, Mrs Marwood, leave the stage before the play's conclusion, neither expressing guilt nor seeking forgiveness.

Fainall is a gambler. When the play opens Mirabell congratulates him on his success, but as the plot unfolds we see that Fainall, although sharper and more literate than Witwoud, Petulant or Sir Willful, is no true match for Mirabell. Mirabell outwits him in the matter of the control of Mrs Fainall's fortune and also in his attempt to fleece Lady Wishfort and her family. In addition—though it is Mrs Marwood who first encourages him to blackmail Lady Wishfort and suggests a plan to him when he does not act on his own initiative—in dictating terms to his mother-in-law he acts the bully. And, like all bullies, he panics when he is himself confronted and attacked. It is ironic that, after sneering at Sir Willful for making an unsophisticated attempt to preserve Lady Wishfort's honour, he then attacks his own wife, trying to kill her. For all his pretence of cynical indifference he is ultimately very much at the mercy of his own uncontrolled emotions.

Fainall's relationships with women are more callous, more self-seeking than those of Mirabell. Contrast, for instance, Fainall's relationship with Mrs Marwood with that between Mirabell and Millamant. Jealousy, mistrust and mutual criticism make the former an uneasy pair. Fainall certainly says he loves his mistress, and fights the idea of losing her, and yet her acid comments create a negative impression. Fainall, trying to justify himself to Mrs Marwood, says that he only married an heiress so that he should have money to squander on her. But Mrs Marwood accuses him of squandering her own money. Crude disagreements of this kind, with each suspecting the other capable of lying, are a very long way from the happier exchanges of Mirabell and Millamant which lead to increasing frankness. Whereas the conversational intimacy of the hero and heroine is leading to a permanent union, it is almost impossible to imagine that Fainall's deliberately secretive obsession with Mrs Marwood will develop in any positive way. He is frightened by her threat to disclose their affair.

Fainall's fear that he will lose his mistress prompts him to declare that he will divorce his wife and marry Mrs Marwood. Mirabell, however, indicates that Mrs Fainall will, in fact, be able to retain and control her husband when he finds that she is in charge of her fortune. Fainall will be too greedy, too materialistic to resist accepting her money on her terms.

Mirabell

Mirabell is the hero: he has enough goodness for his failings to be for-given, enough cleverness to ensure he gets his own way without destroying the family unit. He manipulates other characters into actually wanting him to marry Millamant and get her money. An astute judge of character, he never allows himself to be threatened (as Waitwell and Foible are) but is continually planning and thinking ahead. Thus he is creative and flexible in dealing with his own destiny, defining what he wants and then getting it.

Charming and yet fully in control of events, he is Congreve's arche-typal wit. Effective in debate, he is quick-witted, sharp, and to the point. See, for example, how he criticises Petulant for confusing wit with ignorance and bad manners. Mirabell is adept at adapting another's speech to his own, ironic advantage. This is seen in his satirical use of Fainall's already cynical phrase 'the way of the world', and also in his skilful recognition and capping of Millamant's quota-tion from Waller's 'The Story of Phoebus and Daphne, applied'.

Millamant alone is able to beat him at his own game. Indeed she teases him with being too pompous, too serious. Mirabell complains that she is too capricious, and yet it is this very whirlwind capricious-ness which magnetically attracts him. When he tries to be objective and isolate her faults, he simply finds he has become accustomed to them, and is more in love with her than ever. He sums up his dilemma in an evocative image:

> A Fellow that lives in a Windmill, has not a more whimsical Dwelling than the Heart of a Man that is lodg'd in a Woman. There is no point of the Compass to which they cannot turn, and by which they are not turn'd; and by one as well as another; for Motion not Method is their Occupation. (II. 1. 440–4)

Mirabell, however, is reasonable in his demands when he and Milla-mant discuss marriage. He strikes a cautious note. He is against extremism where drugs and alcohol are concerned, does not want Millamant to disguise her face with make-up, or follow current fashions to the extent of wearing tight corsets which will deform his 'Boy'. Remarks like these show that he is indeed serious about marry-ing Millamant and having an heir, whereas, in the past, he had obviously been equally certain that he did not want to marry Mrs Fainall (then the widow Arabella Languish) when she thought that she was pregnant with his child. Mirabell did, however, go to great lengths to arrange that she should marry someone else. (In the context of the Restoration theatre a move like this was considered more considerate than cynical.) Mirabell's manoeuvres to win Millamant are equally effective. For, at the beginning of the play, he complains that she had paid him minimal attention for fear of antagonising her aunt, but by the end of the play he has persuaded her to act with him in managing Sir Willful and then circumventing her aunt.

Millamant, who loves Mirabell very deeply, pays tribute to his irresistible charm. Many of Congreve's other characters help to build up the same impression. Fainall's and Witwoud's respect, for example, contributes to Mirabell's reputation as a gallant, a chivalrous man-about-town. Foible, too, refers to him as a sweet, winning gentleman. Lady Wishfort, her daughter and Mrs Marwood are all similarly attracted. Indeed it is the bitter fury of Mrs Marwood's discovery that her passion is not returned which makes her turn against her rival's family.

Where, however, Mrs Marwood has only one ally, Fainall, Congreve's hero manages to win over virtually the whole cast as the play progresses. Not only his own servant works for him, but Lady Wishfort's maid also; and, in addition to the help of his future wife, he has that of his ex-mistress. Similarly, Witwoud and Petulant have witnessed his crucial Deed of Settlement.

It is in having secured this crucial legal document, and in having made Waitwell marry Foible before he impersonates Sir Rowland, that Mirabell proves that he can make use of the law of the land to secure his own ambitions and to protect his friends. Thus Mirabell's opening statement 'You are a fortunate Man, Mr Fainall' has been ironically reversed. Of these two gamblers it is Mirabell who is finally successful. He wins the woman he loves, as well as wealth and control over the Wishfort family. Mirabell has achieved this by knowing when to be generous, as, for example, when he returns the Deed of Settlement to his ex-mistress, so that in future she can manipulate her wayward husband. It is significant that it is Mirabell, Congreve's mouthpiece, who concludes the play with the author's ultimate warning: '...Marriage Frauds too oft are paid in kind.'

Witwoud

First introduced in the chocolate house, where he has been gambling with his friend Petulant, Witwoud reveals his easy-going nature, his desire—and his inability—to keep up with the sharper wits of Fainall and Mirabell. We learn that he is a member of Lady Wishfort's intimate circle (she is his aunt), and that he affects a fashionable interest in Millamant, whom he later accompanies in St James's Park. Next seen at Lady Wishfort's, he refuses to acknowledge his half-brother, Sir Willful Witwoud, remarking that it is not fashionable to acknowledge relatives in Town.

His disdain for his dull but virtuous rural relative (which is reciprocated) provides a continuous source of humour. Witwoud's original desire to come to London and escape from his former guardian, Sir Willful, led him to become apprenticed to a lawyer, and then to give up the idea of work altogether, adopting a self-consciously decadent pose. More a type than a rounded, full personality, Witwoud fits in with Congreve's aim, expressed in his Dedication, of creating characters whose humour lies in a consciously adopted rather than naturally inherited weakness. Witwoud's follies are artificial, carefully cultivated. He symbolises fashionable pretension, and because this is a perennial weakness, Witwoud becomes a perennial source of amusement.

Witwoud is criticised by Fainall and Mirabell for his would-be witticisms. They attack his lack of memory, his habit of retailing scraps of other people's conversations, his preference for similes (also attacked by Millamant) and his general love of flowery talk (deprecated by Petulant). Yet, despite his own limitations, he is aware of many other people's shortcomings. He underlines Mincing's affectation and Lady Wishfort's verbosity. He is capable of making mocking and imaginative remarks. His comments on his friend Petulant's three lady visitors are successfully derogatory. His admirable self-mocking remark at the end of the play sums up his own confusion to perfection. He is, he says, like a dog in a dancing school.

Apart from acting as a foil to Sir Willful, Witwoud combines with Petulant to form a comic chorus, the former verbose, the latter inarticulate. Witwoud good-naturedly over-values his friend's testy insults. They decide to go to the park together to insult the ladies, and Witwoud spurs Petulant into being rude to Sir Willful. The pair of them get Sir Willful drunk for Fainall—just as they had both signed the original deed of settlement for Mirabell, although, characteristically, unaware of its contents.

Witwoud's dramatic role, then, is a minor one. Thus his pursuit of Millamant adds to the general impression that she is greatly admired, but, although he plays the courtier, he admits privately that he finds her changeability more disquieting than attractive. But although always a minor character as far as the action is concerned, he occupies a major role in terms of the play's theme. As his name suggests, he represents the foolishness of pretending to be wiser than one is.

Petulant

As his name suggests, Petulant is irritable, impatient and sullen in a peevish, capricious way. A minor character unrelated to the central family of Witwouds, he is Witwoud's friend and foil. They are a comedy team together. Witwoud suggests this with his ironic remark that they agree in the main, like treble and bass. But where Witwoud is good-natured and verbose, Petulant is his opposite—irritable and taciturn. They contradict each other like 'two battledores', as Witwoud constantly 'interprets' his friend's remarks. He helps, with Mirabell and Fainall, to establish Petulant's vices before he appears on stage. In short Petulant lacks judgement, good manners, courage, education, vocabulary, and he is in addition brash, vain, contradictory, impudent and a total liar. Always the more aggressive of the two, he bluntly derides Witwoud as soft and silly, an annihilator of sense.

Petulant is funny because he cannot laugh at himself. He is also funny because he tries to act as a man of the world without understanding true wit, genuine sophistication, and also because he puts great energy into pointless activities. Thus we learn, from Witwoud, that Petulant is accustomed to slip away from a public place, rush home, disguise himself, and then come to 'call' on himself (sometimes even leaving notes) all in an effort to prove his enormous popularity. His equally elaborate manoeuvre, that of paying three whores to hire a coach and follow him pretending to be great ladies avid to see him, is another device, this time to prove his popularity with the opposite sex. His mental limitations are seen early in the play when he tells Mirabell of the plot for Sir Rowland to marry Millamant, little realising that this story originated with Mirabell, who had thought it up as a cover for his own complex plot.

Petulant's vanity is clearly illustrated by the way he informs Mirabell that the ladies did not tell him all their secrets because they feared his malicious charm. It is ironic that he should be so proud of his insulting, boorish ways when his insensitivity cuts him off from society. Witwoud alone interprets his rude outbursts as fire and wit; others are more objective. Mirabell, criticising the way he embarrasses women by shouting obscenities at them, remarks

> Where Modesty's ill Manners, 'tis but fit
> That Impudence and Malice pass for Wit. (I. 1. 480–1)

Even Millamant, who is usually in control of her emotions, says that she has been provoked 'into a flame' by Petulant. She is repelled both by his contradictory nature and by his lack of learning: 'I wonder at the Impudence of any illiterate Man, to offer to make Love'.

Petulant's insensitivity and irritability are best seen when Witwoud encourages him to insult a new arrival at Lady Wishfort's house, his rural relative Sir Willful Witwoud. Petulant deprecates the latter's travel-stained boots and horse by remarking 'Your Horse is an Ass, Sir!' As he gets drunk Petulant becomes increasingly ridiculous. We hear from Witwoud that Petulant and Sir Willful were like two spluttering roasting apples—so cross, they could not get a word out, let alone decide what to quarrel about. Petulant, however, later states that their quarrel was about Millamant. In telling Millamant of this he is hardly the most exciting of lovers: 'If you can love me, dear Nymph— say it—and that's the Conclusion—pass on, or pass off,—that's all.' His clumsy proposal, so different from Mirabell's, emphasises the hero's sophistication. Petulant is no romantic: 'Go flea Dogs, and read Romances', he says to Witwoud, 'I'll go to bed to my Maid.'

In Petulant Congreve creates a character whose crudities are a cause of amusement because we come to anticipate them. Both as a lover and a general conversationalist Petulant is always abrupt. He reduces everything to his own simplistic terms. At the conclusion of this most complex play we find not only that he has signed a legal document without understanding a word of it, but that his comprehension of what has just taken place is equally limited. His final comment, when Sir Willful asks Petulant and Witwoud to accompany him on his travels abroad, is absurd: 'For my part, I say little—I think things are best off or on.' As always, he is gloriously out of tune.

Sir Willful Witwoud

Sir Willful Witwoud's character is a variation on the rustic idiot, a well-known comic type created, for example, by William Shakespeare (1564–1616) in *A Midsummer Night's Dream* (1595/6). But where Shakespeare used rustics such as Bottom to provide strong contrasts with aristocratic and supernatural beings, Congreve used Sir Willful more as a variation on a theme, that of would-be wits. For, while he has some learning, referring for example to Pylades and Orestes, figures from Greek mythology, Sir Willful, as his name suggests, stubbornly wants to be thought a wit. And it is very telling that our first, and last, piece of information about him concerns his desire to go on a cultural tour of Europe, then known as the Grand Tour, the accepted climax of every young gentleman's worldly education. It is ironic, however, that Sir Willful is already forty when he comes to Town to learn some French before setting off on his travels. They have, Congreve implies, been postponed so long that they may never take place.

Sir Willful can be compared with Petulant (who is at times stubborn, grumpy and slow to react) and also with Witwoud, his half-brother. Congreve exploits the irony of two half-brothers having developed so differently: one has provincial values and manners, the other urban. Sir Willful, 'Brother Willful of Salop', has solid moral values, but he lacks mental agility and polish. Witwoud, on the other hand, has frivolity and cynicism but lacks common sense. He is all pulp, where his half-brother is all core. In their exchanges Witwoud can be heartless

—refusing to recognise his relative, for example, because it is not the fashion in Town to do so—but his former guardian is bluntly realistic. 'Fashion's a Fool', he says, and criticises his younger half-brother for having ceased to write normal, informative letters to his friends in Shropshire now that he has become such a fop. He is surprised at Town ways, such as the late hour at which his aunt Lady Wishfort gets up, just as she is shocked by his readiness to pull off his boots in company.

Sir Willful's speech reveals his character. The author gives him simple rural expressions; he mentions a hare's scut, for example. He repeats phrases to gain a point, as in his conversations with Petulant and Fainall, and reacts very openly when he is teased. He is utterly confused by Millamant, because, with his practical and literal mind, he is unable to follow her more fanciful train of thought, or pick up her quotations.

His temperament is contradictory. Shy in the presence of ladies, as when his aunt pushes him into courting Millamant, Sir Willful can also become boisterously uninhibited. See, for example, how when drunk he later sings and jokes and evinces interest in her Ladyship's maids.

Sir Willful Witwoud is basically a good, if limited, man. Middle-aged himself, he nevertheless sides with the younger lovers in trying to win old Lady Wishfort's approval for their marriage. Willful realises that he would hardly make a fitting husband for such a beautiful young woman as Millamant, and that his more spirited and cultured friend Mirabell is much the more suitable man. He makes no claims on her fortune, and his sympathy makes him easy for Mirabell to manipulate —firstly into saying that he will marry Millamant, and later into renouncing her. Sir Willful has other good instincts. He is generous, for example, in trying to defend his aunt from Fainall, and in persuading her to be forgiving. Similarly he includes Witwoud and Petulant in his plans for travel, and at the end of the play he is the one to suggest a dance—a symbol of harmony.

Waitwell

As his name suggests, Waitwell is a reliable servant. Whatever his own inclinations, and they are very human, he remains loyal to his master's considerable commands. Mirabell sets him to impersonate an uncle, Sir Rowland, who is to tell Lady Wishfort that he is a childless bachelor who wishes to marry and thus to prevent Mirabell from inheriting his fortune. Waitwell is used to deceive Lady Wishfort into an embarrassing position from which Mirabell intends to release her on his own terms.

In the first act we hear of Waitwell's marriage. Waitwell, who enjoys innuendoes, is amorous as well as dutiful; in the second act he tells us that he and Foible have been 'solacing in lawful Delights'. He is frivolous about the plot altering him out of recognition: 'The difficulty will be how to recover my Acquaintance and Familiarity with my former self; and fall from my Transformation to a Reformation into Waitwell.'

His next entry is as Sir Rowland, Foible having reassured Lady Wishfort that he is a 'brisk' lover. His gallant speeches, combined with his pretended haste to revenge himself on his 'nephew' Mirabell, work wonders. Lady Wishfort has difficulty in restraining herself. He is ironic about the situation, confessing in secret that he finds Lady Wishfort the 'Antidote to Desire', telling Foible that he would rather carry a sedan chair in the hottest days of summer than continue to play this part for another twenty-four hours. His private sentiments, however, are forgotten when Lady Wishfort reappears with a letter revealing that he is an impostor. Quick to save his own skin, Waitwell acts on Foible's fear that this letter is from Mrs Marwood; he pretends to be jealous of another man, taking up Foible's suggestion of blaming the whole thing on his 'nephew' Mirabell. Hypocritically impersonating a devoted and hot-blooded lover by saying that he could happily die to prove his 'Truth and Innocence', Waitwell leaves to procure a black box containing the writings of his whole estate to convince his mistress of his fidelity. For the moment he has enthralled his buxom widow, promising to return with a marriage contract before the night is over.

Congreve lets us see Lady Wishfort seriously interested in this pretended lover; but his part diminishes as her love turns to hate. He is imprisoned by Fainall, rescued by Mirabell and (after Lady Wishfort has been pacified by Mirabell) reappears with the black box which is so vital in establishing his master's integrity.

Lady Wishfort

Lady Wishfort is the head of her family. She is in charge of Millamant's fortune, and she and her daughter, Mrs Fainall, are also wealthy. Thus when Mirabell wants to secure Millamant—and her fortune—he has to gain Lady Wishfort's approval, and in order to do so he has to understand her character. Similarly, when Mrs Marwood and Fainall try to gain control of her, and her family's money, they also play on the weak points of her character.

What makes Lady Wishfort vulnerable? She is a snob, gullible, old, and desperate to get a husband. Mirabell's plot, embarrassing her by threatening to expose the fact that she has fallen in love with an aristocrat who turns out to be a servant in disguise, threatens all her weak points. Fainall's blackmail, however, relies on her fear of a scandal if her daughter's affair is publicly revealed.

Congreve stresses her social and sexual hypocrisy, slowly building up our anticipation as the play progresses, before actually bringing her on stage. The same is true of her meeting with 'Sir Rowland', which provides the climax to her elaborate preparations for catching a husband. In the episode with Sir Rowland her pomposity (symbolised by her repetitious 'As I am a Person') and her excitement are nicely blended. Anxious to build up an image of lady-like behaviour, she attempts to keep her appetites under control, saying, for example, that she will agree to marry Sir Rowland in order to save his life. Similarly ironic is her display of moralistic books, and her directive to the maid to hide the bottle under the table.

Lady Wishfort is a stock figure: that of an ageing lady chasing the opposite sex indiscriminately, although men do not find her attractive. Mrs Fainall and Mirabell, for example, discuss her in general terms as a type well known to the audience, and the fact that Mirabell was able to win her affections so easily suggests that her predictable reaction to the prospect of another suitor will ensure the success of his plot.

Although she is basically a stock figure, Congreve makes Lady Wishfort memorable. Emotional, changeable, gossiping, verbose, she produces picturesque images, reminding Foible, for example, that she had rescued her from a shop no bigger than a bird-cage. She can occasionally be realistic as when, for instance, she cracks her make-up by frowning and compares her face to an old, peeled wall, or, on a deeper level, sees clearly that Sir Willful will not make a suitable husband for Millamant.

Generally, however, she is easily influenced by others, such as her servant, Foible, or her hypocritical friend, Mrs Marwood. The latter persuades her to consider Sir Willful as a potential husband for Millamant, later encouraging her to submit to the extravagant demands of her son-in-law Fainall. Not only is she slow to realise other people's trickery, but is bad at defending herself whenever she does so. It is significant that when Fainall starts to blackmail her she dreams of a pastoral escape. And, on hearing of her daughter's affair, she absurdly denies any responsibility for her action—having brought her daughter up with no knowledge of or contact with men, and then married her off to a man with the inspiring name of Languish. This can hardly have been the wisest way of helping her to independent survival in a society where the position of women was not easy.

Congreve's concluding image of this comic figure brings home the fact that the action has taken place in a single day; it is convincing that Lady Wishfort, the oldest person, is also the most exhausted. Vulnerable and manipulated throughout the play, she is now protected by Mirabell's good will, but still able to delude herself. Thus she interprets the fact that a scandal has been averted (over her daughter's earlier relationship with Mirabell) as proof of her daughter's innocence. She adds to this irony by convincing herself that this is a measure of her own worth, saying to Mrs Fainall that it is plain she has inherited her 'Mother's Prudence'.

Millamant

Millamant is a beauty, an heiress and a wit. She is Congreve's heroine, well matched with Mirabell. Unlike the other main characters she does not seem to have been scandalously involved with other people before falling in love with him. Her love for Mirabell is her main consideration. But although she loves him and enjoys the power of holding him captive she wants to keep him on her own terms. She wants to marry him, to have as secure a marriage as possible, and, at the same time, to retain as much of her personal freedom as she can. She is, ultimately, a very serious character who has thought out her future and is working to achieve her aims.

Millamant's chief charm, however, lies in the fact that she is never tedious, never boring. She jokes about what deeply matters to her, in the process captivating her audience—both on stage and off it. It is significant that the only person to express reservations about her is Witwoud, the would-be wit, who acts the courtier but is, in fact, somewhat disconcerted by such a genuine humorist. Her light touch is in the best tradition of English literature, from Shakespeare's many comic heroines to Jane Austen's. Essentially sincere, but superficially ironic, Millamant is always unexpected. She does not suffer fools gladly (becoming tired of Petulant's brash illiteracy and Witwoud's similes) but is quite realistic about herself—if Mirabell does not prove a good husband to her she will be, in her own words, a lost thing.

She works, however, to prevent this happening. In the famous 'proviso' scene she lays down conditions for her, and his, future happiness, accepting his ideas about their future. Millamant thinks that they should not be ostentatious about their love, but protect it with privacy. He should not take her for granted but respect her right to make her own decisions about a host of domestic and social matters. After captivating him with her changeability and style Millamant flirtatiously discusses marriage before agreeing, as she puts it, to dwindle into a wife. Her caution pays off. Mirabell's obvious, spontaneous love has no bounds. He will not, as he did with Mrs Fainall, leave her when she becomes pregnant. He looks forward, on the contrary, to her bearing his son. She expects to be faithful to him. Their flippancy is a superficial shield for their developing trust in each other.

It is in her exchanges with Mirabell—in St James's Park, and at Lady Wishfort's house—that Millamant is at her most whimsical, absurd and teasing. She enjoys her confrontations with Mirabell. Satirising a rustic, like Sir Willful, or fighting with a rival, like Mrs Marwood, she can be equally sharp-tongued but less joyous. Congreve suggests her beauty—as he builds up to her grand entrance, heralded, significantly, by her adoring lover, Mirabell—but it is always more than physical beauty which makes his heroine exciting; her repartee—no doubt very carefully written by Congreve—suggests the spontaneous sparkle of original wit.

Millamant does not play a major role in the machinations of the plot. We learn from Mirabell that she has been restrained on meeting him in her aunt's company, a restraint due, he suggests, to her desire not to offend Lady Wishfort who, after all, controls her fortune. Millamant is aware, through Foible, of Mirabell's plot but does little to help him until the play ends. She is, however, very much more than the usual prize for a traditional hero. Rich, beautiful and sophisticated, she is very much a person in her own right.

Mrs Marwood

'Hell hath no fury like a woman scorned.' This phrase from another of Congreve's plays sums up one of the motives behind Mrs Marwood's continually vicious behaviour. We learn from Fainall and Millamant, for example, that Mrs Marwood was responsible for exposing Mirabell's pretended courtship of Lady Wishfort as false. Fainall accuses his mistress of wanting to 'undeceive the credulous Aunt, and be the officious Obstacle of his Match with Millamant'. Then, after hearing that Mrs Fainall had had an affair with Mirabell and that Mirabell had no interest in herself, Mrs Marwood reacts again. She decides not to act generously like Mrs Fainall but to be as vicious as she can. Spurned by jealousy she first tries to make the foolish Lady Wishfort marry her younger rival off to the unsophisticated countryman, Sir Willful Witwoud, but later thinks up a more venomous plot. Pretending to love Fainall, she stirs him into action against Mirabell and his prospective new family.

As well as suffering from her jealousy, Mrs Marwood is basically unhappy. She does not love herself, and consequently sees the world as disgusting, expecting others to act unpleasantly and having no reason for not doing so herself. She is a source of discontent. She is also highly emotional. Her emotional changes, unlike Millamant's, are sinister. She cannot control her negative instincts or the destructive forces at work within her. She is indeed a 'mischievous Devil' but one who is also her own worst enemy.

Her affair with Fainall, which started before he married, is crucial to our understanding of her character and yet—like everything connected with Mrs Marwood—very hard to unravel. We are given no informa-tion about her past, let alone what attracted her to Fainall, why she became involved with him, or exactly what she expected from him. She is particularly hard to follow when she discusses morally ambiguous subjects such as the correct way for her to behave towards Fainall's wife. Self-justification, hypocrisy, and swift attack are all her trade-marks, which we also see in her crafty exchanges on mankind in general, and Mirabell in particular, with both Mrs Fainall and Milla-mant. The one thing which is clear is that Mrs Marwood resents the facts that Fainall has squandered her money.

It is her idea that he should blackmail Lady Wishfort, trying to bully her into handing over all the family assets lest her daughter's affair with Fainall become common knowledge. She herself sends Lady Wishfort an 'anonymous' letter to inform her of Mirabell's strategy over 'Sir Rowland', and later persuades her trusting friend to give in to Fainall's demands by painting a gruesome picture of the law courts and journalists at work. Her own fear of scandal varies. She threatens Fainall with exposing the injuries he has done her, though in the process she will be exposed herself. She does not hesitate to reveal another scandal to help her to get her own way, telling Fainall he is a cuckold so that she can manipulate him all the better. And she says she does not care if her plots are discovered, so long as she is successful. By the end of the action, however, when Foible and Mincing reveal that they found Mrs Marwood in a compromising situation with Fainall, she denies that she tried to swear them to secrecy.

Although Mrs Marwood can be ambiguous, she is nevertheless con-vincing. Her hate, recriminations and desire to be free of an odiously possessive lover are evocatively caught in her first scene alone with Fainall. It is clear that her hatred is indeed love souring, as her expecta-tions have not been fulfilled; but it is not absolutely certain what she wants, or, indeed, if she knows what she wants when she says it is 'not yet too late . . . to loath, detest, abhor Mankind, my self and the whole treacherous World.' And, although some of her speeches are hard to interpret, especially as she does not trust anyone, her final message is a direct threat. When Mrs Fainall comments that she appears to be stif-ling her resentment her enemy savagely replies that 'it shall have Vent —and to your Confusion, or I'll perish in the Attempt'.

Mrs Fainall

Mrs Fainall, Fainall's wife, is Lady Wishfort's daughter, Millamant's cousin, and Mirabell's ex-mistress. Most of her part revolves around her unhappy marriage, and her basically generous instincts towards those who treat her with a degree of kindness. She faces her problems realistically, which lends her some dignity, but is essentially a victim of worldly machinations she is unable to control.

The first conversation between Mirabell and Fainall which informs us that Mrs Fainall is often in her mother's and her associates' company, refers ironically to Fainall's, or his wife's, friend Mrs Marwood and indicates an ambiguous situation. Congreve carefully makes this marriage the subject of innuendo before introducing us to Mrs Fainall and her fashionable friend Mrs Marwood, so that we are ready to question their innocent protestations, to follow their social manoeuvring. Mrs Fainall begins by reviling men: 'Men', she says, 'are ever in Extreams, either doting or averse' (II. 1. 5): her husband is particularly vile. Later, trying to discover the other's real feelings about the opposite sex, Mrs Fainall sees Mrs Marwood change colour after she has mentioned the possibility of marrying Mirabell and astutely reflects that this, in addition to Mrs Marwood's alleged reasons for hating him, hides a secret passion. Mrs Fainall's own social skill at concealing her true feeling is then tested as Mrs Marwood challenges her pretended dislike of Mirabell: she grows pale but neatly blames her embarrassment on her husband's unexpected arrival. Greeting him— 'My soul'—she plays the devoted wife with sarcastic verve; and then directs the conversation so that she can be alone with Mirabell.

Mrs Fainall's insincerity and trickery are no match for her companions however: Fainall has not prevented her departure with Mirabell simply because it suits him to let her go; he is pleased to get rid of her in order to be alone with his mistress. Mrs Marwood is quick to accuse Mrs Fainall of a passion for Mirabell, and Fainall's lack of interest in this accusation shows how calculatingly disinterested he is in his wife: 'And wherefore did I marry, but to make lawful Prize of a rich Widow's Wealth, and squander it on Love and you?' (II. 1. 189). His callousness provokes our sympathy, and we begin to feel the injustice or futility of Mrs Fainall's worldly career,

In her next scene we find her talking to Mirabell, revealing why she married, and at the same time giving us more than a glimpse of a character whose warm and genuine affections made her all the more vulnerable to social hypocrisy. Mrs Fainall married because she was secretly afraid that she was pregnant, and yet the danger of pregnancy came about because she loved and trusted Mirabell. 'Why did you make me marry this Man?' she asks, indicating that Mirabell had no intention of marrying her himself. He craftily fixed up the connection with Fainall 'To save that Idol Reputation'. Manipulated thus, Mrs Fainall wins sympathy because there is no bitterness in her unselfish interest in Mirabell's designs to marry another handsome heiress. It is a tribute indeed that, having once rejected her, Mirabell should then trust her with his plans. Her comments show an astute awareness of the craving for sexual fulfilment and social superiority which make Mirabell's target, her mother, so vulnerable, while her comment— 'Female Frailty!'—shows that she thinks the female sex, generally, grows increasingly pathetic with age.

Foible

Foible, Lady Wishfort's personal maid, is also secretly employed by Mirabell and is essential to his plans. She is a valuable accomplice not only because she follows Mirabell's instructions faithfully but also because she is quick-witted enough to adjust her behaviour (and her husband's) to altering circumstances.

Married to Waitwell, who obviously finds her attractive, she and her husband meet Mirabell to discuss his plan. She has already pretended to Lady Wishfort that Mirabell's uncle Sir Rowland is in love with her (through the device of her having shown him the miniature of Lady Wishfort) and she has also informed Millamant of the plot to manipulate Lady Wishfort by getting the old lady involved with a servant in disguise. Mirabell is more than satisfied, giving her money and promising that she and Waitwell will have a farm if all turns out well.

Foible's adaptability is shown when she rushes back to Lady Wishfort's to find Mrs Marwood has already reported that she has been seen with Mirabell. She persuades Lady Wishfort that she has merely been defending her mistress against Mirabell's slanderous attacks, making use of the old lady's rage to push her still further into the idea of a match with 'Sir Rowland'. She encourages Lady Wishfort to think she is seeking revenge while craftily playing on her vanity, 'your Picture must sit for you, Madam'.

Recounting her ingenious manipulation of these events to Mrs Fainall she praises Mirabell's ex-mistresss for her generosity (unaware that she has been overheard by Mrs Marwood in the closet); she is also instrumental in arranging 'Sir Rowland's' visit to Lady Wishfort, chiding her husband, when they are alone for a moment, when he complains about acting the lover to Lady Wishfort. Subsequently she advises him to seize Mrs Marwood's letter and say that it was written by Mirabell as part of his plotting, thus helping 'Sir Rowland' to escape before her mistress discovers what is going on.

Foible's rise from poverty to the role of trusted confidant is revealed in Lady Wishfort's venomous dismissal of her when, for once, her quick tongue cannot save her, and she fears being sent to prison. Later, however, she saves the day by revealing that she and Mincing know of the adultery of Mrs Marwood and Fainall.

The fact that Mirabell introduces her as a 'penitent' and that she has always been so closely involved in his concerns implies that she and

Waitwell will share in his good fortune (as he had earlier promised). After all, as she had explained to Lady Wishfort, she had made sure that Waitwell was not in any position to do the old lady any permanent harm, by checking the legal aspects of the affair, before meddling in her mistress's business.

Mincing

Mincing, Millamant's servant, is a minor character and a minor source of comedy. She is quick-witted enough to contribute to Millamant's frivolous repartee, as, for example, when she takes up her mistress's suggestion that she had trouble pinning up her hair with prose, after struggling for a whole morning 'Till I had the Cramp in my Fingers, I'll vow Mem. And all to no purpose. But when your Laship pins it up with Poetry, it sits so pleasant the next Day as anything, and is so pure and so crips.' Her pretentions to fashionable chatter and affected pronunciation provide a source of amusement. Witwoud, for example, mimics her: 'Indeed, so crips?'

Mincing is loyal to her mistress and her friends. She is prepared, for example, to 'vouch anything' on Mrs Fainall's behalf without knowing what is required of her. She puts her own ideal of loyalty before mercenary advantage when she publicly describes how Foible and she found Mrs Marwood and Fainall together, preferring to reveal Mrs Marwood's adultery rather than accept the bribes that would, she knows in her wordly wisdom, have been paid to secure a discreet loss of memory.

Peg

Although her role is too minor for her to be listed in the *Dramatis Personae*, Peg provides a variant on the theme of the ignorant person unable to understand or keep up with fashionable allusions. Her naive lack of understanding provokes Lady Wishfort to mounting exasperation. Peg's innocent presentation of a 'cup' of spirits to a determined drinker, eager for alcohol, is followed by her inability to conceal her lack of social hypocrisy when someone calls. 'What', exclaims her fashionable mistress to the 'uncivilised' maid, 'Wou'dst thou go with the bottle in the thy hand like a Tapster?'

Betty

Betty is the serving maid at the chocolate house whose pert remark about the last canonical hour leads on to the servant's report on Waitwell's wedding.

Servant (to Mirabell)

This servant's function is to tell Mirabell that Waitwell and Foible are married, to give him the certificate, and carry a message to Foible.

Servant (to Lady Wishfort)

This servant is witty at Lady Wishfort's expense when he tells Sir Willful that he cannot swear to her face in a morning, before she is dressed, a comment on her use of cosmetics.

Messenger, Coachman and Footman

These characters play a very minor part in the play's machinery.

Part 4

Hints for study

REMEMBER THAT YOU ARE READING A PLAY which the author wrote for the theatre. Try to see it performed if you have the chance. Try reading it aloud, preferably with your friends taking different parts. This will help to make the dialogue come alive, and you will get a sense of how the characters speak to each other.

In reading a play it is often best to read it through first, to get a sense of the dramatic effect, to see how the plot is developed. Then you can go back to a slower, more careful reading, making sure that you understand what the characters say, and why they say what they do, and why they carry out their actions. Remember that you may need to use a dictionary to determine the precise meanings of some words.

Once you have read the play a couple of times see if you can summarise what happens in the different acts. This will give you a sense of the play's structure; you should be able to reconstruct the plot, but, in order to do so, you may need to jot down a rough plan of what occurs in the different acts or scenes. Your notes should provide you with reminders of such things as the nature of the different characters (as expressed in their words and actions) or the kind of society in which the characters live (as expressed in the attitudes of the characters to such things, as, for instance, in *The Way of the World*, reputation, marriage, fortune, or wit). You might consider noting down particular phrases that seem to you to cast a light on the dramatist's intentions.

It is a good idea to consider how you would produce the play on the stage. What parts of the action would move fast, what parts slowly? What items of stage furniture would you need to have? What kind of actors and actresses would you like to play the parts?

When you have to answer examination questions on the play remember to read the examination paper very carefully before choosing which questions you will answer. Make sure you have divided your time sensibly. A few minutes' careful thought before you begin answering will probably mean that you will answer the questions better. And leave time—five minutes at least in a two- or three-hour examination— to re-read your answers and correct any carelessness in the writing. When you have selected your questions be sure you answer what the examiner asks you. Irrelevant matter does not help you to do well, nor does a prepared answer which may not suit the question at all. You need to have your ideas about the play clear in your mind before entering the examination, and you should have made notes when studying the play which will help you later to remember points to support your views. When you have something to say about the play it is sensible to support your argument by mentioning particular parts of the play that are germane to it. You do not need to quote long passages to do this, but you do need to show that you know the text by referring to it.

An examiner will want to be sure that you know the play and that you have formed your own ideas about it rather than taking them from critics. (Remember that an examiner is likely to know where you got your ideas, if they are second-hand ones!) So work out your own ideas about the plot, the characters and their attitudes, and be ready to illustrate them by either brief quotations or references to speeches or actions. If you have time you should try reading other plays of social comedy or what is sometimes called the comedy of manners. You could even try translations of Plautus and Terence to find out what the Romans said about the comic themes of the young against the old, about inheritances, and about servants deceiving their masters or mistresses or their friends or enemies. And you will find that Molière and the French theatre influenced the British Restoration dramatists. If you read other British plays, by say, Dryden, or Wycherley, or Etherege, you will see that there is a certain similarity in all these plays, and this will give you a feeling for what the dramatists' contemporary audiences in the London theatres enjoyed, and what many audiences there and elsewhere have gone on enjoying since. These plays are meant to entertain, though they have often a powerful undercurrent of satire, a desire to expose social hypocrisy.

Quotations

It is useful to pick out some quotations which illustrate points you may wish to make about individual characters, or which may bear upon themes of the play you are studying. You do not need to remember long quotations (and your examiners will be more interested in reading your ideas about the play than in reading long quotations from it). Short quotations will equally well demonstrate your knowledge of the text and your understanding of it. Two sections of quotations follow. Your own choice may be very different, but you should pick out significant remarks as you read the play and note them down.

Quotations indicating character

Mrs Marwood: 'that mischievous Devil'
Mrs Fainall: 'the Pattern of Generosity'

Mirabell:	'You are a gallant Man, Mirabell, and tho' you may have Cruelty enough, not to satisfy a Lady's longing; you have too much Generosity, not to be tender of her Honour'
Millamant:	'What would you give, that you could help loving me?'
	'Well, if Mirabell shou'd not make a good Husband, I am a lost thing'
Fainall:	'Bankrupt in Honour, as indigent of Wealth'
	'Truth and you are inconsistent'
Lady Wishfort:	'that loves Catterwauling better than a Conventicle'
	'As I am a Person'
	'O I'm glad he's a brisk Man'
	'the Antidote to Desire'
Witwoud:	'He has something of good Nature, and does not always want wit.'
Sir Willful Witwoud:	'an odd mixture of Bashfulness and Obstinacy— But when he's Drunk, he's as loving as the Monster in the Tempest'
	'The Fashion's a Fool'
Petulant:	'Where Modesty's ill Manners, 'tis but fit That Impudence and Malice pass for Wit'
Waitwell:	'Married, Knighted and attended all in one Day'
Foible:	'Mrs Engine ... Why this Wench is the *Pass-par-tout*, a very Master-Key to every Body's strong Box.'

Quotations indicating significant themes

The contrast between genuine and superficial wit
'distinguish between the Character of Witwoud and a True Wit'
'to please a Fool is some degree of Folly'

Cynicism and hypocrisy
'What's Integrity to an Opportunity?'
'Why do we daily commit disagreeable and dangerous Actions? To save that Idol Reputation.'

Amorous deceit
'O Man, Man! Woman, Woman!'
'Marriage Frauds too oft are paid in kind.'

Some questions on the play

1. What is meant by a True Wit?
2. Either compare Mrs Marwood and Mrs Fainall, or Mirabell and Fainall.
3. Contrast the relationship of Mrs Marwood and Fainall with that of Millamant and Mirabell.
4. Sum up the relationship between Sir Willful and Witwoud, between Foible and Waitwell, and between Mrs Fainall and Mirabell.
5. Choose a particular series of events and explain why Congreve is a master of comic situation, as, for example, when Mirabell's servant pays court to Lady Wishfort.
6. Explain the values of *The Way of the World*, showing how Congreve adapts traditional themes and archetypal problems.
7. Discuss Congreve's humour and style, indicating why this dramatist thought his last play might attract criticism, and why its wit has been praised for its timelessness.
8. What does Millamant want, how does she go about getting it, and how far do you think she succeeds?
9. What is the legal background to *The Way of the World*?

Answering questions

Planning an answer to question 8: What does Millamant want, how does she go about getting it, and how far do you think she succeeds?

Always plan—in abbreviated form if working at speed—the ideas you want to explain, as for example, in the short argument below which could easily be expanded with relevant incidents and quotations. Devote the same amount of time and effort to each part of a question so that you pick up all the marks available to you. This question is divided into three and so requires three separate answers. Here are three paragraphs which answer the question, point by point.

Millamant wants to marry Mirabell, but on her own terms. She wants to retain elements of her own freedom and individuality after they have married. She wants to keep their love private rather than let it become an empty matter of public display, and she wants their union to last.

She attracts Mirabell not only by her beauty and wit, but by flirting with him until he has been won by her changeable charms. She only agrees to marry him when he accepts her conditions. And, although she appears frivolous, she has obviously considered their future in a practical and realistic way. Once he has agreed to her conditions, she starts to help him to win Lady Wishfort's approval for their marriage.

Congreve's heroine is able to compromise: she accepts Mirabell's provisos as well as making her own conditions. Her perhaps cynical approach and playful bargaining are effective: she wins Mirabell's interest and keeps her self-respect. (Mrs Fainall, who was less cautious, was less successful, being married off to someone else when she thought she was about to bear Mirabell's illegitimate child.) As she is both intelligent and deeply in love, it seems likely that Millamant will continue to fascinate Mirabell.

A suggested essay answer to question 9: What is the legal background to *The Way of the World*?

Legal imagery occurs throughout *The Way of the World*. Like his character Witwoud, Congreve trained in law in London and so had first-hand knowledge of the profession and of its terminology. He includes, for example, mention of *subpoenas* and *noli prosequi*, and cynically describes Lady Wishfort's circle of gossips as a coroner's inquest set up to decide on the week's murdered reputations. Lady Wishfort ironically tells 'Sir Rowland' to beware the law, and later threatens Foible with the law; Fainall seeks recourse to the law to imprison Waitwell; and Mirabell rescues the latter from prison. But Congreve never actually introduces either officers of the law or legal settings, preferring to concentrate on his main family of characters whose images call up the power of the law. Thus Mrs Marwood, for example, highlights the effects of a public trial when she suggests a bloodthirsty 'pack' of bawling lawyers, and Foible's fears conjure up the threat of imprisonment.

The law, however, has deeper uses in this play, for it provides the 'rules of the game' by which various characters try to outwit each other. (There is no comparable religious framework in such a worldly piece.) Congreve neither idealises nor criticises contemporary English law but simply adopts it as the machinery through which his characters can secure their actions. A knowledge of the law helps practical survival in a world where people are forever trying to manipulate each other.

This is a subtle and ruthless drama in which brute force becomes laughable in the face of sophisticated legal manoeuvring. Thus simple Sir Willful's attempt to defend Lady Wishfort with brute strength is sneered at by Fainall, who is using the law to blackmail her, while Fainall's own subsequent attempt to kill Mrs Fainall is seen as a frustrated gesture by someone who has been intellectually outwitted by Mirabell, a man who has made still more cunning use of the law.

Central to the whole play is the concept of the will, for it is the will of Lady Wishfort's late husband which sets the terms of the action. Millamant cannot inherit her six thousand pounds unless Lady Wishfort approves of her marriage. Mirabell manages to get round this clause, by manipulating the law for his own ends. He makes Waitwell marry Foible so that there is no possibility of the false 'Sir Rowland' actually marrying Lady Wishfort and thus gaining control of her and her money. It is Mirabell's possession of a legal document, a Deed of Trust, however, which ultimately gives him power over the others. This, ironically, symbolises his earlier mistrust of Fainall. By obtaining guardianship of Mrs Fainall's fortune prior to her marriage to Fainall, Mirabell has provided her with a safeguard (for which her mother comes to be appropriately grateful). Thus Fainall's attempts to take over his wife's assets with a later Deed of Trust, and his subsequent attempts at blackmail, are foiled, since these assets were already legally in Mirabell's control.

It is significant that Mirabell refers to this clever, if cynical, move as part of 'the way of the world'. He is being ironic at Fainall's expense, quoting him to show that distrust is as common as treachery in a world where widows can make use of the law as an efficient check against future victimisation. Congreve, in addition, ensures that the Fainalls' marriage will be preserved (to prevent a public scandal) as Mrs Fainall (aided by her ex-lover, Mirabell) will be able to use her money to gain control of Fainall. Congreve, in thus using the law to protect both property and private interests, anticipates his own subtle will in which he left his money to the Duchess of Marlborough, which could subsequently be passed to her daughter, the Duchess of Leeds, thus glossing over Congreve's paternity of the girl. Like his hero before him, Congreve adapted public law to secure the ambiguities of private life.

It is significant throughout this play that Congreve's characters equate worth with legal proof, legal assets. Waitwell and Foible are to be rewarded with a lease. Mrs Fainall, asking Mirabell to tell her of his secret plans, hopes she has some degree of credit with him. Similarly, Mrs Marwood, attacking her lover, says that Fainall is as bankrupt in honour as he is indigent of wealth. Marriage is very much a social contract. Thus we have Fainall speaking of having married to make lawful prize of his wife's fortune, and Waitwell mentioning his lawful delights with regard to his bride, Foible, and later—in the character of Sir Rowland—talking not only of fetching legal deeds to prove his worth but of seeking a contract for his proposed marriage to Lady Wishfort. The idea of thrashing out a legal settlement is stressed as Mirabell and Millamant reveal their love—they barter 'Provisos', sealing their 'contract' with a kiss before a 'witness'.

Despite Millamant's attempts to secure future privacy, and

romance, their love will—in a sense—become public property. Their legalised love will serve to cement warring factions as their marriage reinforces social and familial unity.

In conclusion, Congreve's formal legal framework should not be viewed in isolation but in combination with the rules of chance. Fashionable references to gaming and gambling are also stressed. Excitement, risk and danger are summed up by the opening scene where Mirabell and Fainall gamble, Fainall refusing to continue unless Mirabell is really feeling his losses. He does not want to gamble with someone who does not care, any more than he wants to seduce a woman who is not frightened of losing her reputation. Congreve offers the image of gambling as a metaphor for life. The play expands with the idea of Fainall and Mirabell as rival gamblers suffering quick reversals, sudden changes of fortune. Fainall re-establishes the link between gambling and adultery as, for example, when he discusses his wife's secret affair, saying she had 'Pam' in her pocket, as though thinking in terms of card tricks. And at the conclusion of the play Witwoud and Petulant (also originally referred to as gamblers) ask 'who's hand's out?' on seeing the other characters assembled like players at the end of the last act. This phrase, once again, suggests gaming. This time Mirabell is the winner, fate having favoured him. Congreve directs our sympathy towards Millamant, who gambles in agreeing to marriage, fearing that if she looses Mirabell's love she will become a lost thing. Chance and security are never far apart in Congreve's world, as he states in his Prologue—showing that even established authors gamble on the success of each work.

Part 5

Suggestions for further reading

Texts of *The Way of the World*

The Way of the World, 1700; second edition, 1706; included in *The Works*, 3 vols, 1710; reissued as 2nd edition 1717; 3rd edition, 2 vols, 'revis'd by the author', 1719–20.

The Way of the World, ed. K.M. LYNCH (Regents Restoration Drama Series), University of Nebraska Press and Edward Arnold, Lincoln, Nebraska, and London, 1965.

Incognita and The Way of the World, ed. A. NORMAN JEFFARES (Arnold's English Texts), Edward Arnold, London, 1966. This edition uses the second edition of 1706 as copy text, and supplies readings from the first edition of 1700 and *The Works* of 1710. This edition is designed for students.

The Way of the World, ed. BRIAN GIBBONS (New Mermaids Series), Ernest Benn, London, 1971.

The Way of the World, ed. JOHN BARNARD (Fountainwell Drama Texts), Oliver and Boyd, Edinburgh, 1972. This is an old-spelling text, based on the first edition of 1700.

The Way of the World in *Restoration Drama*, vol.4, ed. A. NORMAN JEFFARES, Folio Press, London, 4 vols, 1974. This edition uses the first edition of 1700 as copy text.

Other works by Congreve

Complete Works, ed. M. SUMMERS, Nonesuch Press, London, 4 vols, 1923.

Comedies, ed. BONAMY DOBREE (World's Classics), Oxford University Press, London, 1925. This is based on the text in *The Works*, 1710.

Mourning Bride, Poems and Miscellanies, ed. BONAMY DOBRÉE (World's Classics), Oxford University Press, London, 1928.

Works, ed. F.W. BATESON, Peter Davies, London, 1930.

Letters and Documents, ed. J.C. HODGES, Harcourt Brace and World, New York, 1964.

Complete Plays, ed. H.J. DAVIS, University of Chicago Press, Chicago and London, 1966.

Criticism and biography

ARCHER, WILLIAM: *The Old Drama and the New*, Heinemann, London, 1929.

DOBRÉE, BONAMY: *William Congreve* (Writers and their Work), Longmans, London (for the British Council), 1963.

HAZLITT, WILLIAM: *Lectures on the English Comic Writers* in *Complete Works*, vol.VI, ed. P.P. HOWE, Dent, London, 1930–34.

HODGES, J.C.: *William Congreve the Man: a Biography from New Sources*, Modern Language Association of America, New York, 1941

HOLLAND, NORMAN N.: *The First Modern Comedies: the Significance of Etherege, Wycherley, and Congreve*, Harvard University Press, Cambridge, Massachusetts, 1959.

LAMB, CHARLES: 'On the Artificial Comedy of the Last Century', *The Essays of Elia*, London, 1823.

LYNCH, K.M.: *The Social Mode of Restoration Comedy*, University of Michigan Press, New York, 1926.
A Congreve Gallery, Harvard University Press, Cambridge, Massachusetts, 1957.

MUESCHKE, PAUL AND MIRIAM: *A New View of Congreve's Way of the World*, University of Michigan Press, Ann Arbor, 1958.

MUIR, KENNETH: 'The Comedies of William Congreve' (Stratford-upon-Avon Studies), *Restoration Theatre*, Edward Arnold, London, 1965.

NETTLETON, G.H.: *English Drama of the Restoration and Eighteenth Century*, Macmillan, New York, 1914.

NOVAK, M.E.: *William Congreve*, Twayne, New York, 1971.

SMITH, J.H.: *The Gay Couple in Restoration Drama*, Harvard University Press, Cambridge, Massachusetts, 1948.

WILSON, J.H.: *The Court Wits of the Restoration*, Harvard University Press, Cambridge, Massachusetts, 1948.

The author of these notes

Bo Jeffares was educated at the University of Reading, the Courtauld Institute and Trinity College, Dublin. She has taught English at Trinity College Dublin, History of Art at the University of Stirling, and English at Tamagawa University, Japan. She is married to Masaru Sekine and lives in Tokyo. Her publications include *Landscape Painting* (1979) and *The Artist in Nineteenth Century Fiction* (1979); she has written the York Notes on Sheridan, *The School for Scandal*, and Stevenson, *Treasure Island*.

York Notes: list of titles

CHINUA ACHEBE
A Man of the People
Arrow of God
Things Fall Apart

EDWARD ALBEE
Who's Afraid of Virginia Woolf?

ELECHI AMADI
The Concubine

ANONYMOUS
Beowulf
Everyman

JOHN ARDEN
Serjeant Musgrave's Dance

AYI KWEI ARMAH
The Beautyful Ones Are Not Yet Born

W. H. AUDEN
Selected Poems

JANE AUSTEN
Emma
Mansfield Park
Northanger Abbey
Persuasion
Pride and Prejudice
Sense and Sensibility

HONORÉ DE BALZAC
Le Père Goriot

SAMUEL BECKETT
Waiting for Godot

SAUL BELLOW
Henderson, The Rain King

ARNOLD BENNETT
Anna of the Five Towns

WILLIAM BLAKE
Songs of Innocence, Songs of Experience

ROBERT BOLT
A Man For All Seasons

ANNE BRONTË
The Tenant of Wildfell Hall

CHARLOTTE BRONTË
Jane Eyre

EMILY BRONTË
Wuthering Heights

ROBERT BROWNING
Men and Women

JOHN BUCHAN
The Thirty-Nine Steps

JOHN BUNYAN
The Pilgrim's Progress

BYRON
Selected Poems

ALBERT CAMUS
L'Etranger (The Outsider)

GEOFFREY CHAUCER
Prologue to the Canterbury Tales
The Clerk's Tale
The Franklin's Tale
The Knight's Tale
The Merchant's Tale
The Miller's Tale
The Nun's Priest's Tale
The Pardoner's Tale
The Wife of Bath's Tale
Troilus and Criseyde

ANTON CHEKOV
The Cherry Orchard

SAMUEL TAYLOR COLERIDGE
Selected Poems

WILKIE COLLINS
The Moonstone
The Woman in White

SIR ARTHUR CONAN DOYLE
The Hound of the Baskervilles

WILLIAM CONGREVE
The Way of the World

JOSEPH CONRAD
Heart of Darkness
Lord Jim
Nostromo
The Secret Agent
Victory
Youth and *Typhoon*

STEPHEN CRANE
The Red Badge of Courage

BRUCE DAWE
Selected Poems

WALTER DE LA MARE
Selected Poems

DANIEL DEFOE
A Journal of the Plague Year
Moll Flanders
Robinson Crusoe

CHARLES DICKENS
A Tale of Two Cities
Bleak House
David Copperfield
Dombey and Son
Great Expectations
Hard Times
Little Dorrit
Nicholas Nickleby
Oliver Twist
Our Mutual Friend
The Pickwick Papers

EMILY DICKINSON
Selected Poems

JOHN DONNE
Selected Poems

THEODORE DREISER
Sister Carrie

GEORGE ELIOT
Adam Bede
Middlemarch
Silas Marner
The Mill on the Floss

T. S. ELIOT
Four Quartets
Murder in the Cathedral
Selected Poems
The Cocktail Party
The Waste Land

J. G. FARRELL
The Siege of Krishnapur

GEORGE FARQUHAR
The Beaux Stratagem

WILLIAM FAULKNER
Absalom, Absalom!
As I Lay Dying
Go Down, Moses
The Sound and the Fury

HENRY FIELDING
Joseph Andrews
Tom Jones

F. SCOTT FITZGERALD
Tender is the Night
The Great Gatsby

E. M. FORSTER
A Passage to India
Howards End

ATHOL FUGARD
Selected Plays

JOHN GALSWORTHY
Strife

MRS GASKELL
North and South

WILLIAM GOLDING
Lord of the Flies
The Inheritors
The Spire

OLIVER GOLDSMITH
She Stoops to Conquer
The Vicar of Wakefield

ROBERT GRAVES
Goodbye to All That

GRAHAM GREENE
Brighton Rock
The Heart of the Matter
The Power and the Glory

THOMAS HARDY
Far from the Madding Crowd
Jude the Obscure
Selected Poems
Tess of the D'Urbervilles
The Mayor of Casterbridge
The Return of the Native
The Trumpet Major
The Woodlanders
Under the Greenwood Tree

L. P. HARTLEY
The Go-Between
The Shrimp and the Anemone

NATHANIEL HAWTHORNE
The Scarlet Letter

SEAMUS HEANEY
Selected Poems

JOSEPH HELLER
Catch-22

ERNEST HEMINGWAY
A Farewell to Arms
For Whom the Bell Tolls
The African Stories
The Old Man and the Sea

GEORGE HERBERT
Selected Poems

HERMANN HESSE
Steppenwolf

BARRY HINES
Kes

HOMER
The Iliad
The Odyssey

ANTHONY HOPE
The Prisoner of Zenda

GERARD MANLEY HOPKINS
Selected Poems

WILLIAM DEAN HOWELLS
The Rise of Silas Lapham

RICHARD HUGHES
A High Wind in Jamaica

THOMAS HUGHES
Tom Brown's Schooldays

ALDOUS HUXLEY
Brave New World

HENRIK IBSEN
A Doll's House
Ghosts
Hedda Gabler

HENRY JAMES
Daisy Miller
The Ambassadors
The Europeans
The Portrait of a Lady
The Turn of the Screw
Washington Square

SAMUEL JOHNSON
Rasselas

BEN JONSON
The Alchemist
Volpone

JAMES JOYCE
A Portrait of the Artist as a Young Man
Dubliners

JOHN KEATS
Selected Poems

RUDYARD KIPLING
Kim

D. H. LAWRENCE
Sons and Lovers
The Rainbow
Women in Love

CAMARA LAYE
L'Enfant Noir

HARPER LEE
To Kill a Mocking-Bird

LAURIE LEE
Cider with Rosie

THOMAS MANN
Tonio Kröger

CHRISTOPHER MARLOWE
Doctor Faustus
Edward II

ANDREW MARVELL
Selected Poems

W. SOMERSET MAUGHAM
Of Human Bondage
Selected Short Stories

GAVIN MAXWELL
Ring of Bright Water

J. MEADE FALKNER
Moonfleet

HERMAN MELVILLE
Billy Budd
Moby Dick

THOMAS MIDDLETON
Women Beware Women

THOMAS MIDDLETON and WILLIAM ROWLEY
The Changeling

ARTHUR MILLER
Death of a Salesman
The Crucible

JOHN MILTON
Paradise Lost I & II
Paradise Lost IV & IX
Selected Poems

V. S. NAIPAUL
A House for Mr Biswas

SEAN O'CASEY
Juno and the Paycock
The Shadow of a Gunman

GABRIEL OKARA
The Voice

EUGENE O'NEILL
Mourning Becomes Electra

GEORGE ORWELL
Animal Farm
Nineteen Eighty-four

JOHN OSBORNE
Look Back in Anger

WILFRED OWEN
Selected Poems

ALAN PATON
Cry, The Beloved Country

THOMAS LOVE PEACOCK
Nightmare Abbey and *Crotchet Castle*

HAROLD PINTER
The Birthday Party
The Caretaker

PLATO
The Republic

ALEXANDER POPE
Selected Poems

THOMAS PYNCHON
The Crying of Lot 49

SIR WALTER SCOTT
Ivanhoe
Quentin Durward
The Heart of Midlothian
Waverley

PETER SHAFFER
The Royal Hunt of the Sun

WILLIAM SHAKESPEARE
A Midsummer Night's Dream
Antony and Cleopatra
As You Like It
Coriolanus
Cymbeline
Hamlet
Henry IV Part I
Henry IV Part II
Henry V
Julius Caesar
King Lear
Love's Labour Lost
Macbeth
Measure for Measure
Much Ado About Nothing
Othello
Richard II
Richard III
Romeo and Juliet
Sonnets
The Merchant of Venice
The Taming of the Shrew
The Tempest
The Winter's Tale
Troilus and Cressida
Twelfth Night
The Two Gentlemen of Verona

GEORGE BERNARD SHAW
Androcles and the Lion
Arms and the Man
Caesar and Cleopatra
Candida
Major Barbara
Pygmalion
Saint Joan
The Devil's Disciple

MARY SHELLEY
Frankenstein

PERCY BYSSHE SHELLEY
Selected Poems

RICHARD BRINSLEY SHERIDAN
The School for Scandal
The Rivals

WOLE SOYINKA
The Lion and the Jewel
The Road
Three Shorts Plays

EDMUND SPENSER
The Faerie Queene (Book I)

JOHN STEINBECK
Of Mice and Men
The Grapes of Wrath
The Pearl

LAURENCE STERNE
A Sentimental Journey
Tristram Shandy

ROBERT LOUIS STEVENSON
Kidnapped
Treasure Island
Dr Jekyll and Mr Hyde

TOM STOPPARD
Professional Foul
Rosencrantz and Guildenstern are Dead

JONATHAN SWIFT
Gulliver's Travels

JOHN MILLINGTON SYNGE
The Playboy of the Western World

TENNYSON
Selected Poems

W. M. THACKERAY
Vanity Fair

DYLAN THOMAS
Under Milk Wood

EDWARD THOMAS
Selected Poems

FLORA THOMPSON
Lark Rise to Candleford

J. R. R. TOLKIEN
The Hobbit
The Lord of the Rings

CYRIL TOURNEUR
The Revenger's Tragedy

ANTHONY TROLLOPE
Barchester Towers

MARK TWAIN
Huckleberry Finn
Tom Sawyer

JOHN VANBRUGH
The Relapse

VIRGIL
The Aeneid

VOLTAIRE
Candide

EVELYN WAUGH
Decline and Fall
A Handful of Dust

JOHN WEBSTER
The Duchess of Malfi
The White Devil

H. G. WELLS
The History of Mr Polly
The Invisible Man
The War of the Worlds

ARNOLD WESKER
Chips with Everything
Roots

PATRICK WHITE
Voss

OSCAR WILDE
The Importance of Being Earnest

TENNESSEE WILLIAMS
The Glass Menagerie

VIRGINIA WOOLF
Mrs Dalloway
To the Lighthouse

WILLIAM WORDSWORTH
Selected Poems

WILLIAM WYCHERLEY
The Country Wife

W. B. YEATS
Selected Poems